THE REFERENCE SHELF

Vol. 26

No. 3

REPRESENTATIVE AMERICAN SPEECHES: 1953-1954

Edited, and with Introductions,

by

A. CRAIG BAIRD

Department of Speech, State University of Iowa

THE H. W. WILSON COMPANY

NEW YORK   1954

11557

PREFATORY NOTE

REPRESENTATIVE AMERICAN SPEECHES: 1953-54 is the seventeenth in this annual series. Each volume contains some twenty "representative" speeches delivered by Americans, or by others temporarily identified with this country (see, for example, in earlier volumes speeches by Winston Churchill). The seventeen volumes include more than 375 addresses by more than 250 orators.

These speeches are grouped according to subject matter, as International Relations, Domestic Economic-Social Policies, National Ideals, Party Politics, Industry and Labor, Intellectual and Religious Ideals. Students of public address may prefer also an alternate classification based upon the speaker's purposes, the speaking occasions, the speech types and audiences. Such speeches would be classified according to those given before (1) legislatures (Aiken, Butler, Hennings); (2) international deliberative bodies (Eisenhower); (3) political gatherings (Stevenson); (4) professional meetings (Warren); (5) memorial occasions (Bricker); (6) university convocations (Kennan); (7) learned societies (Elmer Davis); (8) court rooms (John Davis, Marshall); (9) business executive dinners (Lewis); (10) community groups (Fairless, Johnston); (11) television audiences (Dulles, Eisenhower, Hobby, Humphrey, Benson, Brownell); (12) religious assemblies (Evans, Pusey, Mann); (13) labor audiences (Meany); (14) meetings that extend greetings and present awards (Hoover).

This editor, as he has stated previously, refuses to categorize the speakers here inserted as the "best" of a period. He labels them as important in their immediate and larger impact on the American audiences. He hopes that each, in smaller or larger measure, influences or reflects the character and trend of the present American political-social-cultural temper. His assumption is that speechmaking is to be judged by its significance as a social force—its impress on history.

The Introduction to each of the seventeen volumes deals with some phase of speech standards and problems of oral communication. The present Introduction attempts to interpret the economic, political, social, and religious trends of the past year as voiced in the speechmaking. Representative speechmaking is thus viewed as helping to reveal the present "American mind."

The brief introduction to each address aims to give the background and some approach to a critical examination of the speaker, occasion, and speech. The student is encouraged to examine in detail the textual authenticity of the speech, its setting, thought, structure, forms of support, language, audience adaptation, delivery, and immediate and later effects.

The biographical notes in the Appendix suggest a more detailed review of the speaker's background and of the experiences that partly account for the character and effectiveness (or deficiencies) of his later speaking.

The Table of Contents of each edition and the Cumulative Author Index at the end of this volume are further aids to a systematic review of speakers and issues since 1937. A survey in the Index of the preachers, military spokesmen, legislative, labor, industrial, educational, and other professional leaders, radio and television speakers, government executives, and other groups should provide a fairly satisfactory preferred list of those orators comprising any one category.

This volume, like the earlier ones, is a reference source, useful both for subject entries and for speeches and speakers to be studied as types. Each volume, in addition to its use as a library reference, is strongly recommended to students of public speaking, extempore speaking, oral and written communication, discussion and debate, speech composition, history and criticism of contemporary American address, social science, and history, as well as to teachers of such subjects.

This editor is grateful to various speakers and publishers for their cooperation in providing authentic texts and in giving permission for reprinting. Specific acknowledgment is made in each case. The editor also appreciates the excellent cooperation of Professor E. C. Mabie and of the Department of Speech at the

State University of Iowa; of Professor Clarence Edney, head of the Department of Speech at Florida State University; of Ralph Ellsworth, Director of Libraries, State University of Iowa and his staff; and of Norman Kilpatrick, Director of Libraries at Florida State University, and the facilities of those libraries.

The editor welcomes any suggestions of public addresses for possible inclusion in these annual collections.

A. CRAIG BAIRD

March 5, 1954

CONTENTS

INTRODUCTION

ISSUES AND SPEAKERS OF 1953

Speechmaking closely mirrors the immediate times and events. The speaker attempts to be spokesman for the thinking of his audience and of the hour. He both reflects the ideas of his immediate and larger community, and in turn initiates new directions for the social thinking and reaction. Time and place affect strongly both his content and his oral methods.

You who read speeches are to identify yourself with the immediate audience concerned with the speaker; to immerse yourself in the economic, social, and other currents that largely account for the attitudes and activities of the orator and of his listeners and observers.

What dominant issues and moods swept America during 1953 and early 1954? To what extent do these forces help to explain the kind and quality of the speaking? Writers who view the scene from within obviously lack full objectivity, and certainly the omniscience to pronounce detached judgment. We hope, nevertheless, to designate the trends and their significance for the history of speechmaking—in this case the record of American speechmaking of 1953 and early 1954.

INTERNATIONAL PROBLEMS

Korea

The outstanding international event of this period, in American eyes, was perhaps the signing of the Korean truce. If peace did not come, the slaughter at least ceased.[1]

After the truce was established, the debate up and down this nation continued. Did the Truman administration invite an

[1] Dwight D. Eisenhower, July 26, 1953, p 19-21; John Foster Dulles, July 26, 1953. (References in this Introduction are to 1953-1954 speeches; pages are noted for those included in this volume.)

unnecessary war in 1950 by implying that we would not defend South Korea? Was the MacArthur dismissal a major blunder politically and militarily? Who won the war? Were the North Koreans and Chinese as decisively defeated as Eisenhower and Dulles seemed to suggest?

The truce soon revealed the stark situation. Though the rival armies withdrew a mile or so, the daily negotiations at Panmunjom bogged down in a welter of Communist propaganda. For the next six months little was done except to exchange prisoners, and wrangle over "those that did not wish to go home." Endless radio and other speeches in this country reviewed the cases of the twenty-one American prisoners of war who finally cast their lot with the enemy. Endless wrangles also continued at Panmunjom over who should attend the peace negotiations. Should the Soviets appear as a neutral, or as "on their side"? After Arthur Dean, our chief negotiator, finally walked out on the barrage of invective, the scene shifted to Europe.[2]

Western Europe

The unsolved political-military problems of Western Europe in grappling with the Soviets in 1951-52, 1952-53, continued in 1953-54. The month-long Berlin Conference made clear to the Western world and the captive nations that the Soviets, guided almost solely by military strategy, would yield not one inch of their entrenched position throughout Central Europe, including their hold on Germany and Austria.[3]

The issue then continued: Would this military occupation policy of the Soviets lead the Western Europeans to early ratification of the European Defense Community? Would France and Germany settle their stakes in the Saar? Would the United States and Great Britain give France sufficient military guarantees so that the French Assembly would "sign up"? Would France

[2] Arthur H. Dean, December 21, 1953.

[3] Henry Cabot Lodge, Jr., August 25, 1953; John Foster Dulles, February 24, 1954, p33-43. See also Dulles' debates against Molotov at Berlin, January 26, February 3, 4, 5, 6, 1954.

work in harness with a rapidly reviving military West Germany? The answer to these questions was clouded.[4]

Thus the European and Korean problems, including the French Indo-China guerrilla and jungle struggle, seven years old, were transferred to the Geneva Conference scheduled for April 26, 1954, with Red China also invited. Meantime Dulles attempted to assure Americans that such prospective meetings in no way implied that the United States would recognize Red China as a *de jure* government, or approve her admission to the United Nations.[5]

International Control of Atomic Power

With the certainty that the Soviet government now had produced hydrogen as well as atomic war weapons, the issue of what the United States should do became daily more acute. How should we save the entire civilized world from hydrogen bomb destruction? President Eisenhower, before the United Nations Assembly, in what was perhaps one of the most important speeches ever delivered by an American president, proposed one solution: the international control of atomic power for peacetime purposes. The hope was that if Russia would enter into such cooperation the military atomic piles might also be diverted to peaceful channels.[6]

DOMESTIC PROBLEMS

Communism

Communism in the United States continued not only as a military and ideological menace, to be dealt with by every legal and security means, but as a politically dramatic issue. A campaign issue in 1952, communism never lost the headlines. Many observers predicted that it would loom large in the 1954 elections.

[4] John Foster Dulles, at Paris, December 14, 1953; Edward R. Murrow, March 9, 1954.
[5] John Foster Dulles, February 24, 1954, p33-43.
[6] Dwight D. Eisenhower, December 8, 1953, p22-32.

The questions continued to be whether the Truman government had been permeated with Communists; what was the number of "subversives" dismissed under the Eisenhower succession; whether the State and other Federal departments were sufficiently alert against these infiltrations; whether the Army (e.g., at Fort Monmouth, New Jersey) was sufficiently aggressive in weeding out bad risks; whether the congressional investigations, chiefly those under Senator Joseph McCarthy, were handled without reasonable protection for the reputation of citizens before they had recourse to legal defense; whether the McCarthy techniques and influence were undermining constitutional freedom and practices, even though "his ends of destroying communism in the United States were by universal agreement laudable." Dramatic was the speech by Attorney General Herbert Brownell, in which he explained that Harry Dexter White, former treasury official and alleged Communist, had been promoted, as an illustration of President Truman's laxity in "betraying the security of the United States." Equally dramatic was the former president's reply over nation-wide radio-television networks.[7]

Equally stirring to the nation-wide observers and listeners was the speech by former President Truman and the Wisconsin senator's reply after the latter's demand for radio-television time to meet the "personal attack" on him.[8]

Party Politics

During this year the nation and the Republican party lost an outstanding leader, "Mr. Republican," Robert Taft, who died in August, 1953.[9]

Hardly had President Eisenhower been inaugurated when the campaign for electing members of Congress in November 1954 got under way. Early in 1954 the rival parties began to level their heavy guns. By February, at Democratic Jackson Day dinners and elsewhere, at Republican Lincoln Day and other

---

[7] Herbert Brownell, Jr., November 6, 1953; Harry S. Truman, November 16, 1953; Ralph Flanders, March 9, 1954.

[8] Joseph McCarthy, November 24, 1953.

[9] John W. Bricker, August 3, 1953, p75-80.

gatherings, the political charges and counter-charges flew thick and fast.[10]

The series of Republican speeches in February which Senators McCarthy and Jenner, among others, gave as they moved across the country were particularly vitriolic.

Constitutional Changes and Interpretations

The so-called Bricker proposal to amend the Federal Constitution, limiting the executive power to make treaties and to enter into international agreements, was hotly but intelligently debated in the Senate for more than a month. It was finally voted down (with one less than the necessary two-thirds for passage) on February 26, 1954. For many months previously many judicial and other bodies had discussed the issue. (One Gallup poll showed that only some 10 per cent of the voters knew what the proposal meant.) The argument provided a rallying point for internationalists and supporters of United Nations (against the amendment) and political conservatives, many legal students, isolationists (for the amendment).[11]

Notable also was the argument before the Supreme Court concerning segregation in public schools, with Thurgood Marshall as leader for non-segregation and John W. Davis in opposition.[12]

Freedom of Thought and Expression

What should be the limits of free investigation and thought? The question continued to echo in the councils of intellectuals and among students of government, school teachers (some of them hard pressed by critics), decriers of "book burning,"

---

[10] Joseph McCarthy, Charlestown, West Virginia, February 4, 1954; Edward Martin, February 10, 1954; Herbert Lehman, Spessard Holland, William Knowland, February 13, 1954; Thomas H. Kuchel, February 12, 1954; Styles Bridges, April 23, 1953; Adlai Stevenson, December 12, 1953, p65-74, and March 6, 1954; Richard Nixon, March 13, 1954.

[11] Thomas H. Kuchel, June 21, 1953; Hugh Butler, January 10, 1954, p 122-7; Alexander Smith, January 27, 1954; Alexander Wiley, Homer Ferguson, Hugh Butler, February 4, 1954; Carl Hayden, Walter George, February 11, 1954; Wayne Morse, February 16, 1954; John W. Bricker, February 19, 1954; William Knowland, February 24, 1954; Price Daniel, Thomas Hennings, February 26, 1954, p 128-30.

[12] Thurgood Marshall, December 7-8, 1953, p 118-21; John W. Davis, December 7, 1953, p 113-17.

strong-minded foes of subversives, and many others who calmly examined decisions and dissenting opinions of the Supreme Court since its inception and who traced Anglo-Saxon civil liberties history.[13]

Foreign Trade

A majority of Republicans in Congress continued their aim and their speechmaking to kill or weaken the Reciprocal Trade Agreements Act. Clarence Randall's Commission on Foreign Economic Policy endorsed the continuation of that act. Many industrialists, labor leaders, and economists supported that position in their speeches. College students, too, had free trade for their debate proposition for 1953-54.[14]

Fiscal Policy and Free Enterprise

The Republican leaders after 1952 committed themselves to balance the budget, hold down the national debt, and reduce taxes. Behind these specific fiscal programs was the general philosophy of encouraging private enterprise. Endless arguments in Congress, over the air, and before professional and popular audiences dealt with these problems. How could excess profits taxes be eliminated and corporation, excise, and individual income taxes be reduced with personal exemptions stepped up—without further unbalancing the national budget, increasing the debt limit, and stimulating more inflation? And how could national economizing be possible in view of the major needs for adequate national defense? And how could we properly control the complicated fiscal program without encroaching on the individual economic freedoms essential to the highest production and industrial efficiency?[15]

[13] George Kennan, May 15, 1953, p 171-9; Elmer Davis, June 8, 1953, p96-111; G. Bromley Oxnam, July 20, 1953; Earl Warren, January 14, 1954, p87-95.

[14] Eric Johnston, September 29, 1953, p 162-70; Samuel Waugh, September 18, 1953; Hubert Humphrey, June 23, 1953.

[15] George Humphrey, June 3, 1953, p45-59; Benjamin Fairless, September 21, 1953, p 131-42; Eric Johnston, September 29, 1953, p 162-70; Erwin Canham, November 18, 1953.

Agriculture, Industrial Management, Labor

Most farmers apparently continued to argue for and demand ninety per cent parity for price supports. Ezra Taft Benson, Secretary of Agriculture, in many speeches, led the attack in favor of "flexible supports" and a freer agricultural economy. Thus the issue promised to become a major factor in the Midwest voting of November 1954.[16]

Management and labor, too, carried on their traditional discussions concerning the virtues and vices of the Taft-Hartley law and the role of high production in the ultimate determination of prices and wages.[17]

Television and Radio

How much did television change political thinking of the masses in the United States during 1953-54? Certainly political speakers exerted tremendous influence over this rapidly expanding medium. Television, for example, continually brought Joseph McCarthy and his investigations of Communists before the public. President Eisenhower appeared with great frequency and effectiveness on television. And Americans, through television, sat in on many sessions of the United Nations.[18]

Many television discussion and talk programs continued to engage large audiences. "Youth Wants to Know," "Answers for Americans," "American Forum of the Air," "Author Meets the Critics," "Life Is Worth Living" (Bishop Fulton J. Sheen), "See it Now" (Edward R. Murrow), "Elmer Davis Comments," illustrated the type and popularity.

Radio talks, too, continued to hold their millions of listeners. "Invitation to Learning," "American Forum of the Air," "Report from Washington," "America's Town Meeting," "National Vespers" (John S. Bonnell), "The Catholic Hour" (Joseph E.

[16] Ezra Taft Benson, June 3, 1953, p45-59.

[17] John L. Lewis, June 5, 1953, p 150-61; James B. Carey, George Meany, September 7, 1953, p 143-9; Walter Reuther, November 30, 1953; Benjamin Fairless, September 21, 1953, p 131-42; Eric Johnston, September 29, 1953, p 162-70; Martin Durkin, September 22, 1953; Richard Nixon, September 23, 1953; James Mitchell, November 18, 1953.

[18] Dwight D. Eisenhower, June 3, 1953, p45-59, and March 15, 1954 (and on many other occasions); Richard Nixon, March 13, 1954; Adlai Stevenson, March 7, 1954.

Manton), "People, Places and Books" (Gilbert Highet), Fulton
Lewis, Jr., John W. Vandercook, Edward R. Murrow, Frank
Edwards, Erwin Canham, Dr. Ralph Sockman, Dr. Billy Graham,
Drew Pearson, George Sokolsky, Walter Winchell, Lowell
Thomas were typical.

Welfare and Social Security

Should the various welfare programs set up by the New
Deal be cut back, left intact, or expanded? Should unemployment insurance be widely extended? Should old age and survivors
insurance be given to the millions not now eligible? Many a
major and minor speaker talked about social security and every
small taxpayer and older citizen did the same. The second session
of the Eighty-third Congress was apparently moving toward
settlement of these questions in a pattern reminiscent of the
New Deal.[19]

Intellectual and Religious Ideals

Educators continued to concern themselves with the direction
and character of education. Were educators free from political
restraints? What of the effectiveness of the school and college
curriculum? Of general education? The future of the humani-
ties? Adult education? [20]

Finally, preachers and other moral leaders continued to ask,
Have American character and ideals declined? Are Americans
losing their sense of moral and ethical responsibility? What
programs and policies shall organized religion follow to increase
genuine religion in America? [21]

Thus by expanding television, by radio, in congressional
committee hearings and on the Senate and House floors, in state
legislative sessions, in churches, lower and higher courts, at

[19] Oveta Culp Hobby, June 3, 1953, p45-59.

[20] George F. Kennan, May 15, 1953, p 171-9; Paul G. Hoffman, June 14,
1953; Gilbert Highet, June 9, 1953; Robert Blakely, June 29, 1953; Robert I.
Gannon, October 10, 1953; Grayson Kirk, December 2, 1953; Virgil Hancher,
November 11, 1953.

[21] Louis Evans, April 5, 1953, p 180-4; Nathan Pusey, September 30, 1953,
p 193-201; Louis A. Weigle, November 8, 1953; Fulton J. Sheen, September 11,
1953; Louis L. Mann, May 31, 1953, p 185-92; James Francis Cardinal McIntyre,
June 7, 1953; L. B. Elson, June 7, 1953; Norman Vincent Peale, February 21,
1954.

business and professional conferences, among school and college students, in villages, on farms, in factories and business centers, in homes and at the thousands of intimate or more formal clubs —wherever Americans, young or old, met one another, these events and issues were orally interpreted or argued. Public opinion developed and American life, always changing, took on a recognizable character.[22]

[22] For a classification of speeches according to occasion rather than according to leading ideas see Prefatory Note, p3-5.

FOREIGN RELATIONS

THE KOREAN ARMISTICE [1]

DWIGHT D. EISENHOWER [2]

President Dwight D. Eisenhower gave this broadcast to the nation from Washington, D.C., on the evening of July 26, 1953. Secretary of State John Foster Dulles followed immediately. The major TV and radio networks carried the addresses. Eisenhower began his message about one hour after the truce was signed at Panmunjom.

The President's brief address was given partly to allay any general impression that this armistice did not make "peace" in the world and partly to warn that in no sense should it lead us to "relax our guard" in a wide demand to "bring the boys home" or otherwise proceed as we did after the armistice of 1945.

My fellow citizens: tonight we greet, with prayers of thanksgiving, the official news that an armistice was signed almost an hour ago in Korea. It will quickly bring to an end the fighting between the United Nations forces and the Communist armies. For this nation the cost of repelling aggression has been high. In thousands of homes it has been incalculable. It has been paid in terms of tragedy.

With special feelings of sorrow—and of solemn gratitude—we think of those who were called upon to lay down their lives in that far-off land to prove once again that only courage and sacrifice can keep freedom alive upon the earth. To the widows and orphans of this war, and to those veterans who bear disabling wounds, America renews tonight her pledge of lasting devotion and care.

Our thoughts turn also to those other Americans wearied by many months of imprisonment behind the enemy lines. The swift return of all of them will bring joy to thousands of families.

[1] Text furnished by the White House with permission for this reprint.
[2] For biographical note, see Appendix.

It will be evidence of good faith on the part of those with whom we have signed this armistice.

Soldiers, sailors and airmen of sixteen different countries have stood as partners beside us throughout these long and bitter months. America's thanks go to each. In this struggle we have seen the United Nations meet the challenge of aggression—not with pathetic words of protest, but with deeds of decisive purpose. It is proper that we salute particularly the valorous armies of the Republic of Korea, for they have done even more than prove their right to freedom. Inspired by President Syngman Rhee, they have given an example of courage and patriotism which again demonstrates that men of the West and men of the East can fight and work and live together side by side in pursuit of a just and noble cause.

And so at long last the carnage of war is to cease and the negotiation of the conference table is to begin. On this Sabbath evening each of us devoutly prays that all nations may come to see the wisdom of composing differences in this fashion before, rather than after, there is resort to brutal and futile battle.

Now as we strive to bring about that wisdom, there is, in this moment of sober satisfaction, one thought that must discipline our emotions and steady our resolution. It is this: We have won an armistice on a single battleground—not peace in the world. We may not now relax our guard nor cease our quest.

Throughout the coming months, during the period of prisoner screening and exchange, and during the possibly longer period of the political conference which looks toward the unification of Korea, we and our United Nations Allies must be vigilant against the possibility of untoward developments.

And, as we do so, we shall fervently strive to insure that this armistice will, in fact, bring free peoples one step nearer to a goal of a world of peace.

My fellow citizens, almost ninety years ago, Abraham Lincoln, at the end of the war, delivered his second inaugural address. At the end of that speech he spoke some words that I think more nearly would express the true feelings of America tonight than would any other words ever spoken or written. You recall them:

> With malice toward none, with charity for all, with firmness in the right as God gives us to see the right, let us strive on to finish the work we are in . . . to do all which may achieve and cherish a just and lasting peace among ourselves and with all nations.

This is our resolve and our dedication.

INTERNATIONAL CONTROL OF ATOMIC POWER FOR PEACEFUL PURPOSES [3]

DWIGHT D. EISENHOWER [4]

President Dwight D. Eisenhower, in this address before the United Nations General Assembly, at New York City on December 8, 1953, proposed a world pool for the development of atomic power for peaceful ends. The dramatic, perhaps unexpected, character of the proposal stirred wide and highly favorable reaction from the political leaders of the world as well as from the millions of Americans and others who listened to and viewed the speaker.

The President that day flew to New York from a Big Three Conference in Bermuda. Prime Ministers Winston Churchill of Britain and Joseph Laniel of France, at Bermuda, had endorsed the address. Eisenhower and his Washington colleagues spent weeks in its preparation. All United States television and radio networks carried the speech, and the Voice of America broadcast it in thirty-three languages, including Russian.

The representatives of the sixty nations in the Assembly Hall, including Andrei Vishinsky, of Russia, applauded the President for a full minute at the conclusion of his thirty-minute presentation. General Assembly President Mrs. Vijaya Pandit, of India, who presided, said that it was a "very fine speech," and that she hoped that the statesmen of the world would give it "serious consideration." Sir Gladwyn Jebb, of Britain, described it as a "noble and moving statement." Similar sentiments were expressed by many other leaders of both American political parties and by those prominent in the world's capitals. Adverse criticism was remarkably absent from the flood of immediate press, radio, or television comment. Students of Eisenhower's speeches were in general agreement that it was perhaps the high-water mark of his public utterances to this date.

What gave the address such distinction? The effectiveness lay partly in the uniqueness and boldness of the proposition itself. It was a proposition that could not be dodged or dismissed without mature explanation. Then, too, the speech had skillful structural development. The introduction and conclusion each served purposes of conciliation, clarification, and direct appeal without tacked-on or primped-up emotional drives. The main body progressed with unity, appropriate selection of ideas and supports, natural order, and effective proportion of

[3] Text furnished by the White House with permission for this reprint.
[4] For biographical note, see Appendix.

treatment. In addition to the ideas and structure, the document had logical completeness. There was blunt and concrete statement of the need for action and measured unfolding of the solution phase.

Another feature of this address was its skillful audience adaptation. Eisenhower in his composition reflected intellectual integrity, sensitiveness to both his American and world audience, good will, and evident reliance upon high moral principle. The language, too, was largely devoid of vocabulary exuberance that might have interfered with ready translation into many tongues. The style was typically American, free from triteness but not obviously rhetorical.

The President was monotonous in his reading rate, inclined to an unbroken pattern of emphasis that did not distinguish major from lesser thought nuances. But the voice and manner conveyed ample force and unmistakable sincerity without acrimony or personality dominance.

Madame President, Members of the General Assembly: When Secretary General Hammarskjold's invitation to address this General Assembly reached me in Bermuda, I was just beginning a series of conferences with the prime ministers and foreign ministers of Great Britain and of France. Our subject was some of the problems that beset our world.

During the remainder of the Bermuda Conference, I had constantly in mind that ahead of me lay a great honor. That honor is mine today as I stand here, privileged to address the General Assembly of the United Nations.

At the same time that I appreciate the distinction of addressing you, I have a sense of exhilaration as I look upon this Assembly.

Never before in history has so much hope for so many people been gathered together in a single organization. Your deliberations and decisions during these somber years have already realized part of those hopes.

But the great tests and the great accomplishments still lie ahead. And in the confident expectation of those accomplishments, I would use the office which, for the time being, I hold, to assure you that the Government of the United States will remain steadfast in its support of this body. This we shall do in the conviction that you will provide a great share of the wisdom, the courage, and the faith which can bring to this world lasting peace for all nations, and happiness and well being for all men.

Clearly, it would not be fitting for me to take this occasion to present to you a unilateral American report on Bermuda. Nevertheless, I assure you that in our deliberations on that lovely island we sought to invoke those same great concepts of universal peace and human dignity which are so cleanly etched in your Charter.

Neither would it be a measure of this great opportunity merely to recite, however hopefully, pious platitudes.

I therefore decided that this occasion warranted my saying to you some of the things that have been on the minds and hearts of my legislative and executive associates and on mine for a great many months—thoughts I had originally planned to say primarily to the American people.

I know that the American people share my deep belief that if a danger exists in the world, it is a danger shared by all—and equally, that if hope exists in the mind of one nation, that hope should be shared by all.

Finally, if there is to be advanced any proposal designed to ease even by the smallest measure the tensions of today's world, what more appropriate audience could there be than the members of the General Assembly of the United Nations?

I feel impelled to speak today in a language that in a sense is new—one which I, who have spent so much of my life in the military profession, would have preferred never to use.

That new language is the language of atomic warfare.

The atomic age has moved forward at such a pace that every citizen of the world should have some comprehension, at least in comparative terms, of the extent of this development, of the utmost significance to every one of us. Clearly, if the peoples of the world are to conduct an intelligent search for peace, they must be armed with the significant facts of today's existence.

My recital of atomic danger and power is necessarily stated in United States terms, for these are the only incontrovertible facts that I know. I need hardly point out to this Assembly, however, that this subject is global, not merely national in character.

On July 16, 1945, the United States set off the world's first atomic explosion.

Since that date in 1945, the United States of America has conducted forty-two test explosions.

Atomic bombs today are more than twenty-five times as powerful as the weapons with which the atomic age dawned, while hydrogen weapons are in the ranges of millions of tons of TNT equivalent.

Today, the United States' stockpile of atomic weapons, which, of course, increases daily, exceeds by many times the explosive equivalent of the total of all bombs and all shells that came from every plane and every gun in every theatre of war in all of the years of World War II.

A single air group, whether afloat or land-based, can now deliver to any reachable target a destructive cargo exceeding in power all the bombs that fell on Britain in all of World War II.

In size and variety, the development of atomic weapons has been no less remarkable. The development has been such that atomic weapons have virtually achieved conventional status within our armed services. In the United States, the Army, the Navy, the Air Force, and the Marine Corps are all capable of putting this weapon to military use.

But the dread secret, and the fearful engines of atomic might, are not ours alone.

In the first place, the secret is possessed by our friends and allies, Great Britain and Canada, whose scientific genius made a tremendous contribution to our original discoveries, and the designs of atomic bombs.

The secret is also known by the Soviet Union.

The Soviet Union has informed us that, over recent years, it has devoted extensive resources to atomic weapons. During this period, the Soviet Union has exploded a series of atomic devices, including at least one involving thermonuclear reactions.

If at one time the United States possessed what might have been called a monopoly of atomic power, that monoply ceased to exist several years ago. Therefore, although our earlier start has permitted us to accumulate what is today a great quantitative advantage, the atomic realities of today comprehend two facts of even greater significance.

First, the knowledge now possessed by several nations will eventually be shared by others—possibly all others.

Second, even a vast superiority in numbers of weapons, and a consequent capability of devastating retaliation, is no preventive, of itself, against the fearful material damage and toll of human lives that would be inflicted by surprise aggression.

The free world, at least dimly aware of these facts, has naturally embarked on a large program of warning and defense systems. That program will be accelerated and expanded.

But let no one think that the expenditure of vast sums for weapons and systems of defense can guarantee absolute safety for the cities and citizens of any nation. The awful arithmetic of the atomic bomb does not permit of any such easy solution. Even against the most powerful defense, an aggressor in possession of the effective minimum number of atomic bombs for a surprise attack could probably place a sufficient number of his bombs on the chosen targets to cause hideous damage.

Should such an atomic attack be launched against the United States, our reactions would be swift and resolute. But for me to say that the defense capabilities of the United States are such that they could inflict terrible losses upon an aggressor—for me to say that the retaliation capabilities of the United States are so great that such an aggressor's land would be laid waste—all this, while fact, is not the true expression of the purpose and the hope of the United States.

To pause there would be to confirm the hopeless finality of a belief that two atomic colossi are doomed malevolently to eye each other indefinitely across a trembling world. To stop there would be to accept helplessly the probability of civilization destroyed—the annihilation of the irreplaceable heritage of mankind handed down to us generation from generation—and the condemnation of mankind to begin all over again the age-old struggle upward from savagery toward decency, and right, and justice.

Surely no sane member of the human race could discover victory in such desolation. Could anyone wish his name to be coupled by history with such human degradation and destruction?

Occasional pages of history do record the faces of the "Great Destroyers" but the whole book of history reveals mankind's never-ending quest for peace, and mankind's God-given capacity to build.

It is with the book of history, and not with isolated pages, that the United States will ever wish to be identified. My country wants to be constructive, not destructive. It wants agreements, not wars, among nations. It wants itself to live in freedom, and in the confidence that the people of every other nation enjoy equally the right of choosing their own way of life.

So my country's purpose is to help us move out of the dark chamber of horrors into the light, to find a way by which the minds of men, the hopes of men, the souls of men everywhere, can move forward toward peace and happiness and well being.

In this quest, I know that we must not lack patience.

I know that in a world divided, such as ours today, salvation cannot be attained by one dramatic act.

I know that many steps will have to be taken over many months before the world can look at itself one day and truly realize that a new climate of mutually peaceful confidence is abroad in the world.

But I know, above all else, that we must start to take these steps—NOW.

The United States and its allies, Great Britain and France, have over the past months tried to take some of these steps. Let no one say that we shun the conference table.

On the record has long stood the request of the United States, Great Britain, and France to negotiate with the Soviet Union the problems of a divided Germany.

On that record has long stood the request of the same three nations to negotiate an Austrian State Treaty.

On the same record still stands the request of the United Nations to negotiate the problems of Korea.

Most recently, we have received from the Soviet Union what is in effect an expression of willingness to hold a Four Power Meeting. Along with our allies, Great Britain and France, we were pleased to see that this note did not contain the unacceptable pre-conditions previously put forward.

As you already know from our joint Bermuda communiqué, the United States, Great Britain, and France have agreed promptly to meet with the Soviet Union.

The Government of the United States approaches this conference with hopeful sincerity. We will bend every effort of our minds to the single purpose of emerging from that conference with tangible results toward peace—the only true way of lessening international tension.

We never have, we never will, propose or suggest that the Soviet Union surrender what is rightfully theirs.

We will never say that the peoples of Russia are an enemy with whom we have no desire ever to deal or mingle in friendly and fruitful relationship.

On the contrary, we hope that this Conference may initiate a relationship with the Soviet Union which will eventually bring about a free intermingling of the peoples of the East and of the West—the one sure, human way of developing the understanding required for confident and peaceful relations.

Instead of the discontent which is now settling upon Eastern Germany, occupied Austria, and the countries of Eastern Europe, we seek a harmonious family of free European nations, with none a threat to the other, and least of all a threat to the peoples of Russia.

Beyond the turmoil and strife and misery of Asia, we seek peaceful opportunity for these peoples to develop their natural resources and to elevate their lives.

These are not idle words or shallow visions. Behind them lies a story of nations lately come to independence, not as a result of war, but through free grant or peaceful negotiation. There is a record, already written, of assistance gladly given by nations of the West to needy peoples, and to those suffering the temporary effects of famine, drought, and natural disaster.

These are deeds of peace. They speak more loudly than promises or protestations of peaceful intent.

But I do not wish to rest either upon the reiteration of past proposals or the restatement of past deeds. The gravity of the time is such that every new avenue of peace, no matter how dimly discernible, should be explored.

There is at least one new avenue of peace which has not yet been well explored—an avenue now laid out by the General Assembly of the United Nations.

In its resolution of November 18, 1953, this General Assembly suggested—and I quote—

that the Disarmament Commission study the desirability of establishing a sub-committee consisting of representatives of the Powers principally involved, which should seek in private an acceptable solution . . . and report on such a solution to the General Assembly and to the Security Council not later than 1 September 1954.

The United States, heeding the suggestion of the General Assembly of the United Nations, is instantly prepared to meet privately with such other countries as may be "principally involved," to seek "an acceptable solution" to the atomic armaments race which overshadows not only the peace, but the very life, of the world.

We shall carry into these private or diplomatic talks a new conception.

The United States would seek more than the mere reduction or elimination of atomic materials for military purposes.

It is not enough to take this weapon out of the hands of the soldiers. It must be put into the hands of those who will know how to strip its military casing and adapt it to the arts of peace.

The United States knows that if the fearful trend of atomic military buildup can be reversed, this greatest of destructive forces can be developed into a great boon, for the benefit of all mankind.

The United States knows that peaceful power from atomic energy is no dream of the future. That capability, already proved, is here—now—today. Who can doubt, if the entire body of the world's scientists and engineers had adequate amounts of fissionable material with which to test and develop their ideas, that this capability would rapidly be transformed into universal, efficient, and economic usage.

To hasten the day when fear of the atom will begin to disappear from the minds of people, and the governments of the East and West, there are certain steps that can be taken now.

I therefore make the following proposals:

The Governments principally involved, to the extent permitted by elementary prudence, to begin now and continue to make joint contributions from their stockpiles of normal uranium and fissionable materials to an International Atomic Energy Agency. We would expect that such an agency would be set up under the aegis of the United Nations.

The ratios of contributions, the procedures and other details would properly be within the scope of the "private conversations" I have referred to earlier.

The United States is prepared to undertake these explorations in good faith. Any partner of the United States acting in the same good faith will find the United States a not unreasonable or ungenerous associate.

Undoubtedly initial and early contributions to this plan would be small in quantity. However, the proposal has the great virtue that it can be undertaken without the irritations and mutual suspicions incident to any attempt to set up a completely acceptable system of world-wide inspection and control.

The Atomic Energy Agency could be made responsible for the impounding, storage, and protection of the contributed fissionable and other materials. The ingenuity of our scientists will provide special safe conditions under which such a bank of fissionable material can be made essentially immune to surprise seizure.

The more important responsibility of this Atomic Energy Agency would be to devise methods whereby this fissionable material would be allocated to serve the peaceful pursuits of mankind. Experts would be mobilized to apply atomic energy to the needs of agriculture, medicine, and other peaceful activities. A special purpose would be to provide abundant electrical energy in the power-starved areas of the world. Thus the contributing powers would be dedicating some of their strength to serve the needs rather than the fears of mankind.

The United States would be more than willing—it would be proud to take up with others "principally involved" the development of plans whereby such peaceful use of atomic energy would be expedited.

Of those "principally involved" the Soviet Union must, of course, be one.

I would be prepared to submit to the Congress of the United States, and with every expectation of approval, any such plan that would:

First—encourage world-wide investigation into the most effective peacetime uses of fissionable material, and with the certainty that they had all the material needed for the conduct of all experiments that were appropriate;

Second—begin to diminish the potential destructive power of the world's atomic stockpiles;

Third—allow all peoples of all nations to see that, in this enlightened age, the great powers of the earth, both of the East and of the West, are interested in human aspirations first, rather than in building up the armaments of war;

Fourth—open up a new channel for peaceful discussion, and initiate at least a new approach to the many difficult problems that must be solved in both private and public conversations, if the world is to shake off the inertia imposed by fear, and is to make positive progress toward peace.

Against the dark background of the atomic bomb, the United States does not wish merely to present strength, but also the desire and the hope for peace.

The coming months will be fraught with fateful decisions. In this Assembly; in the capitals and military headquarters of the world; in the hearts of men everywhere, be they governors or governed, may they be the decisions which will lead this world out of fear and into peace.

To the making of these fateful decisions, the United States pledges before you—and therefore before the world—its determination to help solve the fearful atomic dilemma—to devote its entire heart and mind to find the way by which the miraculous inventiveness of man shall not be dedicated to his death, but consecrated to his life.

I again thank the delegates for the great honor they have done me, in inviting me to appear before them, and in listening to me so courteously. Thank you.

THE BERLIN CONFERENCE [5]

JOHN FOSTER DULLES [6]

John Foster Dulles, Secretary of State, reported to the nation, via radio and television, on Wednesday, February 24, 1954, on the Berlin Conference.

That conference, in which the leading participants were Georges Bidault of France, Anthony Eden of Britain, Vyacheslav Molotov of the Soviet Union, and Mr. Dulles, convened from January 25 to February 18. Twenty-seven sessions were held on the problems of Germany, Austria, and Far East and general disarmament. (Six sessions were secret, all on the Far East.) The Communists yielded nothing on the problems of unifying and withdrawing from Germany or Austria.

The conference agreed for the Big Four to meet at Geneva on April 26, to grapple with the issues of Korean peace, and the termination of the eight-years French-Communist war in Indo-China. Communist China, South Korea, and the other belligerents in the Korean war would be invited to participate at Geneva.

Dulles, in this broadcast of February 24, was attempting to clarify the results of his prolonged diplomatic clashes with Molotov concerning the German and Austrian issues, and to justify his approval of including Red China at Geneva.

Despite the forthright explanations of Secretary Dulles, first to the House and Senate Foreign Relations committees and to the leaders of both parties, and secondly to the American public, the national reaction was one of doubt or skepticism concerning the wisdom of parleying with Communist China. Had he opened the door which would make inevitable the recognition of Red China and its admission to the United Nations? Domestic politics would demand no compromise in that direction. Pressure from France and Great Britain, on the other hand, might insist on such recognition. Hence the probable dilemma facing our State Department in the impending deliberations in April.

Mr. Dulles continued in 1954 to demonstrate high qualities of diplomatic leadership. His many extempore replies to Molotov at Berlin, and his series of speeches at home since January 1953 on his international policies stamped him as sound thinker and speaker of marked ability. He is no orator, but he talks with vocal vigor and general animation that have enlisted for him large and growing numbers of followers.[7]

[5] Text furnished by the Department of State.

[6] For biographical note, see Appendix.

[7] For further comment on Dulles as speaker, see *Representative American Speeches:* *1947-48,* "Not War, Not Peace," p58-67; *1949-50,* "North Atlantic Pact," p 15-27; *1950-51,* "United Front Against Red Aggression," p54-64; *1951-52,* Japanese Peace Treaty," p41-7; *1952-53,* "Western European Army," p 15-20.

Last Friday evening I returned to Washington after four weeks of daily discussion at Berlin with the foreign ministers of France, Great Britain and the Soviet Union—Mr. Bidault, Mr. Eden, Mr. Molotov. Also, on the way back, I met with Chancellor Adenauer of Germany.

I find on my return that there is some confusion as to what really happened. That is not surprising. It is difficult to grasp quickly the results of four weeks of debate on many different matters. Indeed, the full results cannot be clearly seen for many months. I can, however, say that this meeting had two results which will profoundly influence the future.

First, as far as Europe was concerned, we brought Mr. Molotov to show Russia's hand. It was seen as a hand that held fast to everything it had, including East Germany and East Austria, and also it sought to grab some more.

Secondly, as far as Korea and Indo-China were concerned, we brought Mr. Molotov to accept a resolution which spelled out the United States position that Red China might in these two instances be dealt with, but not as a government recognized by us.

You may ask whether it was worth while to go to Berlin and to make the great effort that the Conference involved merely to obtain these results.

My answer is yes, and I have no doubt about that. Berlin cleared the way for other things to happen. The unification and the strengthening of West Europe may now go on. In Asia there could be a unification of Korea and an end to aggression in Indo-China—if Red China wants it.

I do not predict that these things will happen. What I do say is that they could *not* have happened had it not been for Berlin.

Five years had elapsed since the Western Ministers had met with the Soviet foreign minister. During those five years much had occurred.

A war had started and been stopped in Korea.

A war had reached ominous proportions in Indo-China.

Stalin had died and his successors talked more softly.

Six nations of Europe had created their Coal and Steel Community and planned to move on to a European Defense Community.

Communist China had emerged as an aggressive military organization, allying its vast manpower with that of the Soviet Union.

In the Soviet Union itself, industrial and agricultural strains were developing.

In East Germany, the spontaneous outbreak of June 17, 1953, revealed, in one enlightening flash, how much the captives crave freedom.

What did all of this add up to, in terms of world politics? Many speculated and no one knew. The uncertainty was leading to hesitation, wishful thinking and some paralysis of action.

There was only one way to find out—that was to meet with the Russians and deal with them in terms of some practical tests.

We went to Berlin in the hope that Soviet policies would now permit the unification of Germany in freedom, or at least the liberation of Austria. Those two matters would, in relation to Europe, test the Soviet temper. We hoped to achieve those two results and we were determined to let no minor obstacles defer us.

The obstacles we incurred were, however, not minor, but fundamental.

The Soviet position was not at first openly revealed. It was masked behind ambiguous words and phrases. But as the Conference unfolded and as Mr. Molotov was compelled to respond to our probing of his words, the Soviet purpose became apparent.

The seating and speaking order at the Conference table were such that it always fell to me to speak first after Mr. Molotov. Then after me came Mr. Bidault of France, and then Mr. Eden of Britain. They carried with conspicuous ability their share of the task. Between the three of us, we exposed what lay behind Mr. Molotov's clever words. For the first time in five years the people of West Europe, America, and indeed all who could and would observe, sized up today's Soviet policy out of Mr. Molotov's own mouth, instead of by guess or by theory.

It amounted to this: To hold on to East Germany; To permit its unification with West Germany only under conditions such that the Communists would control the election machinery through all Germany; To maintain Soviet troops indefinitely in Austria; To offer Western Europe, as the price of Soviet "good will," a Soviet-controlled Europe which would exclude the United States except in the nominal role of an "observer" along with Communist China.

This last Soviet project for what Mr. Molotov called "European security" was so preposterous that when he read it laughter rippled around the Western sides of the table to the dismay of the Communist delegation.

Laughter is a denial of fear and the destroyer of mystery—two weapons upon which the Soviet Union has relied far too long. Both of these weapons were swept aside in one moment of Western laughter.

But Mr. Molotov did more than just to furnish us with an occasion for ridicule. In that same breath, he told Germany that the price of unification was total Sovietization. He told Austria she was to be occupied until Germany paid the Soviet price. He told France that the western frontier of communism was to be the Rhine and not the Elbe. He told all Western Europe, including the United Kingdom, that the price of momentary respite was for the Americans to go home.

His final utterances were harsh. When he called for the abandonment of a European Defense Community, the dismantling of the North Atlantic Treaty Organization, the scrapping of United States bases, he spoke with no soft words. Gone was the post-Stalin "new look." Thus he made clear what, to some, had been in doubt.

The Soviet position admitted of no real negotiation. There is no middle ground between free German elections and the kind of elections which were carried out in the Eastern Zone of Germany, where the people were forced to deposit Communist party ballots bearing one set of names alone.

There is no middle ground between a free and independent Austria and an Austria infiltrated with Russian soldiers.

There is no middle ground between an Atlantic community defense system and "Americans, go home."

There is no middle ground between freedom and slavery.

For the clearest and sharpest and simplest exposition of these basic truths, all of us are indebted to Mr. Molotov.

In my closing statement before the conference last Thursday afternoon, I recalled that we had fought the Second World War for goals expressed in the Atlantic Charter, to which the Soviet Union had subscribed. One of these was "freedom from fear." But, once victory was won, the dominant Soviet motive had been "fear of freedom."

There is no doubt in my mind that the Soviet leaders genuinely fear freedom. They do not feel safe unless freedom is extinguished, or is defenseless. That Soviet attitude made it impossible to achieve any agreement at Berlin in relation to European matters.

I have referred to the efforts of the Western ministers to require Mr. Molotov to expose Soviet policies in their reality. That effort gave drama to every meeting of the four. There was another aspect which carried, too, its drama. That was the effort of Mr. Molotov to divide the three Western powers.

Mr. Molotov occasionally complained that he was at a disadvantage because we were three to his one. But from his standpoint, that was an advantage. It is much easier to divide three than it is to divide one. If Mr. Molotov had achieved that division, he would have won the Conference. In that respect, he failed totally. The Conference ended with a greater degree of unity between the three western powers than had existed when the Conference began.

That unity did not come about merely because there had been prior planning. There had been able planning, and our United States staff was one of which all Americans can be proud. But no planning could anticipate all the moves which could be made by so shrewd a diplomat as Mr. Molotov and which called for instantaneous response. The unity that emerged was a natural and spontaneous unity which came from the fact that the three foreign ministers stood for governments and nations which were dedicated to the concepts of human liberty and national integrity which Mr. Molotov attacked.

It is a tragedy for the peoples of Germany that Germany and Berlin must remain divided; and for the people of Austria that they remain occupied and economically exploited. It can be said, however, to the eternal honor of these peoples, that they would not have had us do other than we did.

The Austrian bipartisan delegation offered the Soviet Union every concession compatible with national honor. They firmly refused to go beyond that point.

We were constantly in contact with the government and political leaders of the Federal Republic of Germany and we knew that they did not want us to buy German unity at the price of making Germany a Soviet satellite. The Germans under Soviet rule had no government to represent them, but we saw them in East Berlin. They provided a startling and shocking contrast with the people of West Berlin. There we saw open countenances and everywhere welcoming smiles and gestures. In the Soviet sector of Berlin we saw only frozen and haggard countenances, as the people stood silently under the vigilant eyes of the ever-present and heavily armed police. A few waved at me from behind a policeman's back and many wrote me through underground channels. They made clear that they passionately wanted unification with West Germany, but they did not seek that unification on terms which would not really have ended their own enslavement, but would have merely extended that enslavement to their brothers of the West.

The alien peoples under Soviet rule can know that nothing that happened in Berlin has made less likely the unification of Germany, or the liberation of Austria and indeed the restoration of freedom to Poland, Czechoslovakia and the other satellite countries. At Berlin I did not conceal my views in this respect. In my closing remarks to the three other foreign ministers I said, "We do not believe that the peoples of Germany or Austria or for that matter of other neighboring nations need to bury their hopes."

I am confident that in saying this I expressed the abiding sentiments of the American people.

The governments of France and Britain rejected, without hesitation, the Soviet proffer of European "peace" at a price which would have meant Western European disunity in the face of the huge consolidation of Soviet power.

Thus it came about that, in relation to Europe, much has been revealed. The Soviet has offered its alternatives to Western planning and they are so repellent that there seems no choice but to proceed as planned. Certainly, that is the United States' conviction.

I had two private talks with Mr. Molotov about advancing President Eisenhower's atomic energy plan. We have agreed on the next procedural step which will involve communication between Moscow and Washington through the Soviet Embassy in Washington. I should note in this connection that the Berlin Conference adopted a resolution to exchange views on limitation of armament as contemplated by a United Nations Resolution of last November. It was, however, made clear that these talks would not replace, or cut across, the independent development of President Eisenhower's atomic energy plan.

We dealt also with the matter of peace in Korea and Indo-China.

We wanted a political conference on Korea because we felt it a duty to ourselves, the Korean people and the United Nations to seek to replace a Korea divided by an armistice with a Korea united in peace. The Korean armistice recommended such a conference with the Communists. But for over six months, the Communists had blocked agreement upon either the time or place or composition of that conference. As far back as last September, in agreement with President Rhee of Korea, the United States had proposed that the conference be held at Geneva. That proposal had been rejected. We proposed, also in agreement with President Rhee, that the conference should be composed of Communist China, Soviet Russia, North Korea, and, on the United Nations side, the Republic of Korea, and the sixteen United Nations members which had fought in Korea. This proposal had been rejected. The Communists insisted that a group of Asian "neutrals" should be present and that Soviet Russia would be among these "neutrals" and so not bound by conference decisions.

We were able at Berlin to settle all these matters. It was agreed that a conference will be held at Geneva, as we had long ago proposed, and that the composition will be precisely that which the United States, the Republic of Korea and the United Nations General Assembly had sought. There will be no Asian "neutrals" there.

Some profess to fear that the holding of this conference will imply United States recognition of Communist China. That fear is without basis. Those throughout the world who suggest that the prospective Geneva conference implies recognition are giving the Communists a success which they could not win at Berlin. The Resolution adopted at Berlin explicitly provides—I shall read the text—

It is understood that neither the invitation to, nor the holding of, the above-mentioned conference shall be deemed to imply diplomatic recognition in any case where it has not already been accorded.

I had told Mr. Molotov, flatly, that I would not agree to meet with the Chinese Communists unless it was expressly agreed and put in writing that no United States recognition would be involved.

Mr. Molotov resisted that provision to the last. He sought by every artifice and device, directly and through our allies, to tempt us to meet with Communist China as one of five great powers. We refused, and our British and French allies stood with us. When we went into the final session last Thursday afternoon, I did not know what Mr. Molotov's final position would be. So far, he had not accepted my position. We were to adjourn at seven o'clock. At six o'clock—just sixty minutes before the final adjournment—Mr. Molotov announced that he would accept our non-recognition proviso.

A Soviet concession of that order ought not to be ignored.

My basic position with reference to Communist China was made clear beyond the possibility of misunderstanding.

In my opening statement (January 26), I said

I should like to state here, plainly and unequivocally, what the Soviet Foreign Minister already knows—the United States will not agree to join in a five-power conference with the Chinese Communist aggressors for the purpose of dealing generally with the peace of the world. The United States refuses not because, as is suggested, it denies that the regime exists or that it has power. We in the United States well know that it exists and has power because its aggressive armies joined with the North Korean aggressors to kill and wound 150,000 Americans. . . . We do not refuse to deal with it where occasion requires. . . . It is, however, one thing to recognize evil as a fact. It is another thing to take evil to one's breast and call it good.

That explains our non-recognition of the Communist regime and also our opposition to its admission to the United Nations.

I adhered to that position without compromise. It is that position which is reflected in the final Berlin Conference Resolution. Under that Resolution the Communist regime will not come to Geneva to be honored by us, but rather to account before the bar of world opinion.

The Berlin Resolution also touches on Indo-China. It says that "the establishment, by peaceful means, of a united and independent Korea would be an important factor . . . in restoring peace in other parts of Asia," and it concludes that "the problem of restoring peace in Indo-China will also be discussed at the conference."

This portion of the Resolution was primarily and properly the responsibility of France. The United States has a very vital interest in developments in this area and we are helping the French Union forces to defeat Communist aggression by helping them out with grants of money and equipment.

But the French and peoples of the Associated States of Indo-china are doing the actual fighting in a war now in its eighth year. They have our confidence and our support. We can give counsel and that counsel is welcomed and taken into account. But just as the United States had a special position in relation to the Korean armistice so France has a special position in Indo-China.

I recognize, of course, that the Soviet Union would not have accepted, 100 per cent, our terms for the Korean political conference, unless it expected to benefit thereby. But so do we.

I can think of some Soviet benefits that we would not like and should prevent. But I do not wholly exclude the idea that the Soviet Union might in fact want peace in Asia.

We can hope so, and we shall see. In the meantime, we shall keep on our guard.

There is, however, no reason why we should refuse to seek peacefully the results we want merely because of fear that we will be outmaneuvered at the conference table. No informed observers believe that we were outmaneuvered at Berlin.

We need not, out of fright, lay down the tools of diplomacy and the possibilities which they provide. Our cause is not so poor, and our capacity not so low, that our nation must seek security by sulking in its tent.

Berlin gave the free nations up-to-date, first hand, post-Stalin knowledge of Soviet intentions. That knowledge was not reassuring. It shows that the free nations must remain steadfast in their unity and steadfast in their determination to build military strength and human welfare to the point where aggression is deterred and the ideals of freedom are dynamic in the world.

We must continue to hold fast to the conviction that the peoples and nations who are today not the masters of their own destinies shall become their own masters.

If we do all of this, not belligerently, but wisely and soberly; if we remain ever watchful for a sign from the Soviet rulers that they realize that freedom is not something to be frightened by, but something to be accepted, then we may indeed, as these eventful coming months unfold, advance the hopes for peace of the world, hopes so eloquently voiced by President Eisenhower last April, and again last December.

In all of this, we Americans have a special responsibility.

Over recent years, the fearful problem of dealing with Soviet expansion has brought many to a truly disturbing emotional and moral state. In a sense, brains have been washed to such an extent that many are tempted to trade principles of justice for some sense of momentary respite.

Our ultimate reliance is not dollars, is not guided missiles, is not weapons of mass destruction. The ultimate weapon is moral principle.

George Washington, in his farewell address, called upon our nation to observe justice toward all others.

> It will [he said] be worthy of a free, enlightened, and, at no distant period, a great nation to give to mankind the too novel example of a people always guided by an exalted justice. . . . The experiment, at least, is recommended.

That recommendation has, in fact, guided us throughout most of our national life and we have become the great nation which Washington foresaw. This is not the moment to forsake that guiding principle. It is not a moment to flee from opportunities because we fear that we shall be inadequate. If what we stand for is right, why should we fear?

There are some in Europe who would have us forsake our friends in Asia in the hope of gain for Europe. There are some in Asia who would have us forsake our friends in Europe in hope of gain for Asia. We dare not be critical of them, for they are subject to strains which we are spared by our fortunate material and geographical position. Indeed, there are some Americans who would have us sacrifice our friends both in Asia and in Europe for some fancied benefit to ourselves.

I do not argue that American foreign policy should be conducted for the benefit of others. American foreign policy should be designed to promote American welfare. But we can know that our own welfare would not really be promoted by cynical conduct which defies moral principles. In a world in which no nation can live alone, to treat our friends unjustly is to destroy ourselves. We must stand as a solid rock of principle on which others can depend. That will be the case if we follow George Washington's advice and continue to be a people who are guided by "exalted justice."

DOMESTIC ECONOMIC–SOCIAL POLICIES

KEEPING THE GOVERNMENT
HOUSE IN ORDER [1]

Dwight D. Eisenhower, George M. Humphrey, Oveta
Culp Hobby, Ezra Taft Benson and
Herbert Brownell, Jr. [2]

President Dwight D. Eisenhower and four of his cabinet members—George M. Humphrey, of the Treasury Department, Oveta Culp Hobby, Secretary of Health, Education and Welfare, Ezra Taft Benson, Secretary of Agriculture, and Herbert Brownell, Jr., Attorney General, presented this television report to the nation on the evening of June 3, 1953. It was the first program exclusively on television from the White House. It was an experiment to acquaint the national masses with the problem of "keeping the government's house in order." More specifically this television broadcast aimed to reassure the electorate of the nation concerning the leadership of the Republican administration after six months in office.

The program was geared to secure maximum audience attention and response. The advertising agency of Batten, Barton, Durstine and Osborn provided the technical assistance in the lighting, exhibits, and other details of the thirty-minute "show." (This firm has been responsible for the Jack Benny, Groucho Marx, "Your Hit Parade," and other shows.) White House Secretary James Hagerty told reporters that the firm had nothing to do with the content. The broadcasting pattern was that of a panel symposium with each of the five speakers taking his turn and following up with brief dialogue. The President was master of ceremonies. His were preliminary, introductory, and final remarks.

The usual television techniques were much in evidence. The aim was to have "spontaneous and unrehearsed" performance. But the script was carefully written and rewritten. At least two full dress rehearsals were held.

The President through his language and manner attempted to create a "homey" atmosphere, to make the entire treatment so simple that the ordinary listener-viewer would understand all, and in addition would be

---

[1] Text furnished with permission for this reprinting through the courtesy of James C. Hagerty, Press Secretary to the President.
[2] For biographical note in each case, see Appendix.

interested. Especially were the opening remarks framed to "catch" and hold the average televiewer.

What of the net effect? Ben Duffy, of the advertising agency, pronounced it "one of our best shows." Reaction was along party lines. Republicans in Congress praised the TV venture and Democrats reserved judgment. Six months later the experiment had not been repeated.

Some parts of the panel were too "slick," whereas others, those of Benson and Brownell, were weighted with too many facts and propositions to be readily assimilable. In view of the controversial issues identified with each of these major departments, it was felt that too many cabinet speakers were involved in this twenty-eight minute show. The President and his fellow speakers had to rely more on prestige than on sustained argument to carry their point on this network occasion. With Brownell, Benson, and Humphrey especially under fire from many Democrats and some Republican quarters, it is doubtful whether the propagandistic result of this attempt at political popularization was up to the sponsors' expectations.

Good evening, everybody.

This evening some of the Cabinet members have gathered here with me to discuss points of interest—points of interest to your Government and to you.

Now, of course, everybody's first interest is the family, its security and its happiness. Now the security and the happiness of any family depends upon a number of things—the income, to see that the family is well fed and well clothed; that your loved ones are safe no matter where they may be; that the roof is not leaking, and the children are getting educated and that fences on the farm are mended. In short, what you are concerned about is that the house is in good order.

Now, everybody helps to do that—everybody in the family. The Government is no different. Everybody that's in the Government is here to help keep your governmental house in good order, so that you may live the kind of life that you want in this country.

Now, we are concerned, therefore, with the security of the nation—externally and internally—its welfare. Now that security, remember, is not just military. It involves the prosperity of our farmers and the education of our children; it involves spending not more than we take in—live within our means like a family should.

It involves proper protection. Then when you have all of those things you have the Government house in order.

Now, in previous talks I have told you something about this job of protecting the national house from threats abroad—from the threat of communism, what it costs to protect; how we get the money; how we spend it—all of that sort of thing.

I'm going to refer to that no more except to say there is going to be no new Munich and at the same time there is going to be no risk of a general war because a modern war would be too horrible to contemplate.

We are going to keep our temper; we are going to build our strength. I am going over to Bermuda to meet with some of our friends and talk over these things.

But remember in these vast problems that affect every one of our lives, there is no thought that you can cut the knot, you must untie it, slowly and laboriously.

Now, tonight, the group that has gathered here to talk with me about this keeping of your Government house in order are four Cabinet members.

The first one is heading the newest department of Government. It has to do with the welfare and the education and the health of our people. And so as you would imagine it is headed by a woman because that's the woman's job in the home. This is a lady from Texas—Mrs. Hobby.

Next, we have a man whose job it is to keep the finances straightened out—and of course that's a real job. We have for that George Humphrey of Ohio.

Now the next thing we have is a farm problem—and for the Secretary of Agriculture we have a farmer. He is Ezra Benson of Utah.

Finally, we have here this evening to discuss with you some of our problems of internal security, keeping the internal house secure against the boring of subversives and that sort of thing—the head of the Justice Department, the Attorney General, Herbert Brownell.

He is a Nebraska-born, New York lawyer. And that ought to make a good combination for that particular job. Now, in order that we discuss what we know you are interested in, I will show you how we get our ideas.

Over here, in this corner, you see a basket of mail. This is a portion of one day's mail at the White House. We have been averaging over three thousand letters a day in an average week—heavy weeks it's more.

Now from this whole mass, I am going to read to you just parts of one letter, to show you what one citizen in our country is thinking about, and it's sort of a challenging letter.

"Dear Mr. President," this lady from Pawtucket, Rhode Island, writes. "I am writing you to ask some questions that have me deeply worried. I am a housewife with four children, and though I don't know much about the budget you and your people have to worry about, I do know something about running my own family budget. That is why I have so many questions, when I read about all the money you have to spend for guns and planes, and all the problems that you must have when you try to balance our country's budget. The sums are so huge I really find it almost impossible to grasp them."

And I might tell the lady, so do I. "I wonder how you even know where to begin. Won't you please explain to me, in words I can understand, just how you are going to have our money keep its value, and at the same time make our country strong and secure."

I chose that letter because it brings up this great problem of security, and the money that it costs. Now, it's a good starting point and I want to tell you, before Mr. Humphrey takes over to discuss something about finances, we must remember this:

During seventeen of the past twenty years we have gone in debt. Borrowing cheapens money. That's like water in your coffee—it just doesn't go very far and isn't worth much. Now higher prices mean your savings are worthless. So I have asked Mr. Humphrey and our Director of the Budget, Mr. Dodge, to get after this thing and in order to keep spending under the amount we take in so that your dollar will still buy what it should buy. That's his job, and now he is going to tell you about it.

MR. HUMPHREY: Mr. President, I think the woman from Rhode Island was right. I think it is a lot harder, a lot tougher job to balance the national budget than it is your own home budget, because we owe so much money nationally, and we are spending so much money every single year.

Let me just take this chart that I have here and show you where all that money goes to. Seventy-three per cent of the total money we spend goes for defense; 15 per cent goes for fixed charges—that is, things like interest, and all sorts of things that the Congress has voted that we pay, like State aid and all that sort of thing. It only leaves 12 per cent for the ordinary running of the Government.

Now then, our job is to balance this budget. Our job is to get our income even with our outgo. That can be done in two ways, either by raising more taxes or by cutting expenses. Well, of course we don't want to raise taxes—we want to reduce taxes—so the way left is to cut expenses.

And that involves two serious problems. The first problem is that we can't so cut our expenses that we interfere with security. As you have said we have got to maintain the security of this country. The second big problem is this—over the last year or two a great many materials, war materials and other materials, have been bought c.o.d. They are delivered now, as the deliveries come we have to pay for them in cash.

I would just like to show you another chart, here, that will illustrate to you the way in which our spending and our income are growing apart as planned for the next few years—the program that we found when we came. Here you will see this line going way up here is spending, and here you will see this line way down here is income.

In between the two is a widening difference, a widening spread which is a deficit. Now that deficit has got to be stopped. Unless it's stopped, we are going to be right back on the old merry-go-round of inflation.

THE PRESIDENT: Well, now, of course, George, we know we are going to stop it. But as an ex-soldier I have promised the American people two things: They are going to be secure, and, next, these expensive military establishments are going to be maintained in the most economical way possible. You are going to get one dollar's worth for every dollar we spend. And I am going to keep that promise.

MR. HUMPHREY: That's just right, Mr. President. What we are going to do is to cut these expenses slowly. We are going to study every month what can be done. We have made a good start already, but we are going to continue every month as we go along and make further reductions in those expenses.

By that sort of process I think we will be well balanced out by June in 1954, provided we do not have a much worse condition in the world develop. Of course, something could happen in Russia that would upset our plans.

To accomplish that purpose we have set up a new tax bill. Now in that new tax bill, we ask for an extension of the excess profits tax for an additional six months to carry it from July, when it would expire, to the first of January. The reason we do that is because we believe that it is grossly unfair to relieve just a few—the relatively few corporations—who pay an excess profits tax and give them tax relief before we give relief to all the other corporations and to all of the people.

If the Congress will pass the bill that we have before them, the bill that we are recommending to them, with the savings that we have already made, with the savings that we are going to make in the next fourteen months and with this tax money— this excess profits tax money that we can use to reduce the deficit —it will justify a reduction on the first day of January for taxes for all the people of the country—individual tax reductions.

That will mean that everyone will get a tax reduction at the same time. There will be no favorite few. It will help to balance the budget. It will help to stop inflation. It will help to keep sound money. It will help to keep business active, and more jobs, and it will provide better living for all.

THE PRESIDENT: Mr. Secretary, I endorse every single word you say. And you could have added that all of us despise this excess profits tax. It's inequitable, it's unjust, it's clumsy and it's awkward. But, as you say, it must not be taken off until we can reduce the individual income taxes as we should, as quickly as we can get at it.

Now, we know from the mail that we get here, that people are for a decent tax program, to get expenses and outgo in balance; and in those letters we are getting an 8 to 1 vote of confidence for that entire program.

Now, the next person that is going to talk to you is going to talk to the people, particularly, that are key men in our agriculture—the farmers. One out of nine of our wage-earners is a farmer, and when he is in trouble all the nation is in trouble. We are going to get a firsthand picture from Mr. Benson, who, as I told you before, is a farmer himself.

MR. BENSON: Thank you, Mr. President. When you called me to this very tough and difficult job back in December, you asked me if I would be willing to try and serve the American people by being a champion of the farmers. Your Administration had already pledged itself to greater stability in agriculture, increasing the national income and the proportion that goes to farmers, and building a sound program in which the farmers would take part.

Now, I have traveled from one end of the nation to the other in years past and since December, as this little chart will indicate; I have been into most of the agricultural areas, and we have held meetings with farmers; I have addressed them and conversed with them, learned of their problems and listened to their comments and their hopes, and their desires; and in order to get a broad picture of the situation in agriculture today we need to go back to 1947. In that year farmers were receiving good prices, and the relationship between their prices and the prices they had to pay for the things they purchased were favorable.

But since that time there has been a rather rapid decline in farm prices. For the last two years, as this chart will indicate, the trend of prices received by farmers has been downward, while their costs, represented here, have remained relatively high. That means that, as every farmer knows, he has been caught in a squeeze.

However, during the last few months prices have tended to stabilize, as you can see, and the costs have come down somewhat, reducing that squeeze. But during this two-year period— 1951 to 1952—farm prices declined 16 per cent.

THE PRESIDENT: Well, one fellow that's been caught in that squeeze very badly is the cattle raiser, as you and I well know, and we have had many conferences with them.

Now, we must remove that squeeze. We are going to have stability in farm income, and we are going to do it with no farmer being taken over by the Government. We are not going to regiment the farmer.

MR. BENSON: There is another phase of this problem that pertains to our decline in exports, Mr. President. Normally, farmers export about 10 per cent of their total production. That's a very important part. However, there has been a decline in exports in the last two or three years.

Two years ago, for example, we exported about half of our total wheat production. This last year alone there has been a decline of 15 per cent in our exports abroad.

In order for agriculture to be prosperous, it must not only have good markets at home but big markets abroad. And of course this is a two-way road, this foreign trade, so if we sell abroad we must also permit them to sell here. That's why farmers are in favor of the extension of the reciprocal trade program.

Now, usually we think of businessmen and manufacturers as being primarily interested in foreign trade. But I presume the individual who is most deeply concerned with this matter of foreign trade is this man we call the American farmer.

THE PRESIDENT: Now, I think, Mr. Secretary, you should talk just a little bit about our surpluses. We hear a lot about them, and remember, from our viewpoint, it's not just dollars that's here involved—it's the moral values that are involved also.

MR. BENSON: That's very true, Mr. President. At the present time, and for some months, we have been purchasing, as you know, large quantities of products. These have been going into storage. They have been part of the present farm program. Of course, it's a very serious thing when we have large accumulations of burdensome surpluses of farm products.

And so we are beginning, now, to build programs from the grass roots that will prevent unreasonable supplies of these commodities which may result in spoilage and some products becoming rancid. We hope that we can prevent these surpluses and the high cost to the taxpayer resulting therefrom.

We can all remember a few years ago when we had the large surplus of potatoes, which were dyed blue in order to make them unsalable. The answer is not moving products into storage, but into stomachs.

THE PRESIDENT: Well, of course, Mr. Secretary, we do know this: We do need some surpluses. We need surpluses to carry us over from one crop season to another. And we are talking only when these get too large. And here again, the most important part is not the money involved, but I refer again to this business of the moral value.

It's unthinkable, unconscionable, as I see it, that the United States should have wheat molding and crops spoiling, and people —friends of ours—should be starving in the world.

Right now, for example, Pakistan has had a two-year drought, a drought that has been very, very serious. They need a million tons of wheat. And I have already sent to the Congress a measure recommending that we give it to them. And I hope it will be passed soon.

MR. BENSON: In building these farm programs from the grass roots, Mr. President, there are six important basic concepts that should be kept in mind.

In the first place, these programs should build markets and move products into use at fair prices to the farmers.

Secondly, they should permit adjustments in production and give the farmer some freedom in his operations.

Third, programs should not price our products out of the world or domestic markets.

And fourth, they should not hold an umbrella over synthetics and competing products.

And fifth, basic to the whole program is this matter of research and speedy application of it.

And of course, encouragement of a self-help program for the farmers.

THE PRESIDENT: And the only thing that you did not mention that I want to say just a word about, is the research program in agriculture. It is very important. I visited Beltsville the other day, and I saw wonders in research that I wish every one of you could see. It will show you how the farmer is really getting new outlets for his crops.

Now thank you very much, Mr. Benson. Now, we are going to come to the department that deals with health, welfare and education. It's the newest department of Government. You see we have had nine for a long time—nine departments. Now we have got a new one. This is one that Mrs. Hobby heads. I am going to ask her to tell you something about it now. Mrs. Hobby.

MRS. HOBBY: Well, Mr. President, there are so many different activities in our department that touch people, young and old, in public health, in education, pure food and drugs, Social Security, and Children's Bureau, and vocational rehabilitation, that it's difficult, sometimes, to say which problems are the most urgent.

But, in line with your suggestions, we have recently sent three pieces of legislation to the Congress. Two deal with the school situation in the United States. The other piece of legislation deals with the restoration of the right of factory inspection to the Pure Food and Drug.

Shortly we shall send to the Congress a piece of legislation which will extend the coverage of old-age and survivors insurance benefits to millions not now covered. We have had a group of twelve experts studying this problem, and together with Treasury we are developing a simplified plan of tax collection. Our plan would extend coverage to farmers, certain state and local government employees, the self-employed, professional people, domestic workers, farm laborers and others.

Now, we have two laws—or two bills—which relate to the Office of Education. Of course, education is primarily the responsibility of the state and local communities. But there are certain communities in which the Federal Government has created a problem. This occurs in several different ways. One, by removing land from the school tax rolls, and two, by adding student population to the school rolls without taxable property.

This occurs when the parents either live on or work on Federal property. There are notable examples of this situation in Limestone, Maine; in Derby, Kansas; in Piketon, Ohio. Now, the Federal Government recognizes its responsibility and shortly the Congress will start hearings on two bills which will aid these over-crowded school districts—one for construction and the other for maintenance and operation.

THE PRESIDENT: Well, now, Mrs. Hobby, tell us something of that trouble we are having with the Food and Drug Act, will you please?

MRS. HOBBY: Well, Mr. President, that concerns me very much. We have sent to the Congress an amendment to the Pure Food and Drug Law. We believe it is vital to the protection of the American people.

If it is adopted by the Congress, it will restore the right of the Pure Food and Drug to inspect the factories which produce and process food and drugs.

Last fall, the Supreme Court held that the factory inspection language was contradictory, and that the inspectors could enter only when given consent. Fortunately, the great majority of the processors and producers of food and drugs gave consent. But we need the law for those who refuse consent, and refuse to let our inspectors observe their operations and their sanitary conditions.

THE PRESIDENT: Well, I think, Mrs. Hobby, that everybody will agree that you have about as complicated a task as there is in government. You run the biggest insurance business and you run a medical research center, and everything between.

But there is one thing that must give you great satisfaction. You have the department that sort of epitomizes or symbolizes the warm feeling of government for all of our citizens.

And now, my friends, we come to this business of security inside our borders. It's a complicated job because, as we search out those people that are unfit to serve you, we must protect the innocent. That is what we are doing every day.

We go after the weeds of disloyalty, but we don't want to uproot a single good plant. The man at the head of that, as I told you before, is Herbert Brownell. And he is going to tell you about it now, and what he is trying to do in this field.

MR. BROWNELL: In the Department of Justice, Mr. President, we seek to protect the security of our homes—our internal security, through the use of four laws, or programs.

First, we prosecute and jail the leaders of the Communist party in this country, and all those who seek to overthrow our Government by force and violence. We can do that largely because of the fine investigative work of the FBI arm of the Department of Justice under Director J. Edgar Hoover, and we are making good progress on that.

Then, second, we seek to enforce the law which requires agents of foreign governments who are in this country to register and to disclose their finances, and to label their propaganda that they send around to the American people. We are meeting resistance on this, but we intend to pursue it vigorously.

Then, third, under the immigration laws, we are making fine progress on the program of denaturalizing and deporting racketeers and subversives who violated the hospitality of our country, or who got here, in the first place, by false affidavits.

And then, finally, our fourth special tool to protect our internal security, is the employee security program that you spoke about as being a matter of good housekeeping, of weeding out from the Federal payrolls themselves persons who are not good security risks. It went into effect just a few days ago, to replace the old loyalty program which was ineffective.

And it's based on two ideas—one is, that working for the Federal Government is a privilege and not an absolute right, so that the Government is entitled to maintain high standards of trustworthiness in its employees. And the other idea is that there is a great difference between disloyalty and being a security risk; for many of the employees could be a security risk and still not be disloyal or have any traitorous thoughts, but it may be that their personal habits are such that they might be subject to blackmail by people who seek to destroy the safety of our country.

Or they may associate themselves with known subversives. Now you and I, in our private affairs, certainly would not trust our secrets to people that we could not confide in. And the same thing with the National Government. We believe that the tremendously important secrets of our national security should be entrusted only to employees who can guard those secrets in the best interests of the country.

Now, as I say, this program has just gone into effect. But we believe that without fanfare and steadily over the course of the next few months, we will be able to weed out from the Federal payroll every security risk.

THE PRESIDENT: There is one other phase of this thing I wish you would speak about for just a minute, Herb. It is this business of government action in this field going on behind closed doors—what we are doing to bring things out in the open, so that people will know what is going on.

MR. BROWNELL: Well, that is an important function there in the Department of Justice. We have abolished the closed-door policy that we found there.

For example, first in the matter of tax settlements. We now disclose those to the public the minute that they are made so that there will be no temptation for skulduggery or behind-the-closed-doors attitude on the part of the lawyers there in the department.

And second, when it comes to these fraud cases, where people used to come into the department and claim that they were too sick to face the music—that was done behind closed doors.

But now we take them into court, and let the judges appoint an impartial doctor to see whether or not they should stand trial for these frauds.

And finally, in the matter of presidential pardons, we also have abolished the closed-door policy. And when a presidential pardon is granted to anybody who has violated our laws and is incarcerated in our Federal penitentiaries, we disclose that, make it a matter of public record along with the list of sponsors for that pardon.

Now I know you have said to us, and we thoroughly believe there in the department, that one of the most important responsibilities of your Administration is the impartial administration of justice without favoritism. And so we are making that a keystone of the department.

THE PRESIDENT: And I hope, my friends, that you agree that our internal security is in very good hands. And let me make one observation about that before we go further. And it is this: The great mass of your Federal employees are a wonderful, dedicated group of men and women, and whose jobs are going to be protected. He was talking only about those few that damage them.

Now, I know we have not answered your problems this evening, ladies and gentlemen, but I hope you see some of the factors in those problems, and how we are approaching their solution. I hope you will realize that since government is just people, you have seen the kind of people that are trying to solve these things for you.

We have done something, and are doing things to repair the holes in the roof, and keep the fences mended, and keep the industries flourishing, employment high, and the farms productive.

Now, on the defense program, just a word: It is very large, but it is logical. We are not going to cripple this nation, and we are going specifically to keep up its air power. Right now, sixty cents of every dollar that goes into the defense business is in some form of air power or air defense.

Now, we are going to keep reviewing these plans. We are going to report to you from time to time with these, or with other people with me, so that you know what is going on. Because our effort is to secure peace, and prosperity in peace.

My friends, thank you for being with us. Good night. God bless you.

OFF-SHORE OIL BILL [3]

GEORGE D. AIKEN [4]

Senator George D. Aiken (Republican, Vermont) gave this brief speech in the Senate, May 5, 1953, at the end of the long debate on the off-shore oil legislation. The Senate then voted 56 (35 Republicans and 21 Democrats) to 35 to pass the bill, which gave the coastal states title to any submerged lands within their "historic boundaries," land and resources from three to ten and one-half miles seaward.

On May 13, the House approved the Senate measure, and on May 18, President Eisenhower, fulfilling his campaign pledge, signed the document.

This debate covered twenty-five days of actual debate, in addition to weeks of committee consideration. Shortly before his death, the late Senator Taft noted that the opponents had uttered almost a million words and the supporters upwards of 300,000.[5]

The Senate critics of the bill had argued that it was a "giveaway" of from $62 billion to $300 billion worth of oil to Texas, Louisiana, and California, and that the Federal Government was the proper agency to develop the resources of the continental shelf.

Senator Aiken stated the essence of the negative position. His is an excellent example of condensed argument—organized by a series of questions (the issues in the case) and rounded out by a swift statement of his own intended vote.

On March 15, 1954, the Supreme Court ruled, 6 to 2, that Congress had the right to dispose of United States property "without limitation." Justices Douglas and Black dissented and Chief Justice Warren did not participate in the decision.

MR. [JAMES E.] MURRAY [Democrat, Montana]: I yield five minutes to the Senator from Vermont.

MR. AIKEN: Mr. President, like everyone else, I am happy to see this debate come to a close. It has been conducted upon a high level, having been handled admirably by leaders on both sides of the question. The senior Senator from Florida [Mr.

---

[3] *Congressional Record.* 99:4609-10. May 5, 1953 (daily edition). Text and permission for this reprint through the courtesy of Senator Aiken.

[4] For biographical note, see Appendix.

[5] For further comment, see the debate "Tidelands Oil," by Spessard L. Holland and Herbert Lehman, *Representative American Speeches: 1952-53,* p 142-9.

Holland] and the junior Senator from Texas [Mr. Daniel], and the other proponents of the joint resolution, have handled their side of the case skillfully and, at times, convincingly.

However, in the final analysis, the determination of how one will vote on an important matter such as this must be reached in one's own mind. After hearing both sides of the question being presented ably and thoroughly, as they have been, I have asked myself these questions:

First, has Congress the authority to dispose of the lands under the sea which have, for generations, been regarded as belonging to the Federal Government? I have read carefully the testimony given by the Attorney General of the United States before the Committee on Interior and Insular Affairs, and I believe that Mr. Brownell cast sufficient doubt upon the authority of Congress to dispose of those lands to warrant a great deal of hesitation before voting to do so.

The second question I have asked myself is this: If we assume that Congress does have the authority to dispose of these lands and quitclaim them to the states, is such disposal of the lands being made on a fair and equitable basis? When I ask that question, I think of all the other states where there are Federal lands, where there is Federal domain, particularly our western states, and I realize that the income to the states where the lands are located, from leases and royalties on minerals and oil lands in those states is restricted to $37\frac{1}{2}$ per cent. It is planned under Senate Joint Resolution 13 to give to the coastal states 100 per cent of the income from such resources. Certainly if the coastal states are entitled to 100 per cent of the income from the undersea lands, then the inland states are entitled to equitable treatment.

The third question and perhaps the most important, is this: Is the effort to transfer the undersea oil lands from Federal ownership to the ownership of the states a prelude to further raids upon natural resources of the United States by interested groups of people? For many years there has been building up in this country a determination on the part of certain groups to acquire unto themselves the natural resources of the United States which have always belonged to all the people. I think in particular of the plan to raid or to seize Niagara Falls. The efforts now being made to grab the power from the St. Lawrence development, so that instead of all the people getting the benefits, a very few will receive the profits. I think of the proposals to dispose of great public power plants, such as Boulder Dam, Bonneville, Grand Coulee, and even the TVA; and I wonder where we may be headed in that respect. Other groups would take unto themselves the forests on our publicly owned lands and all the minerals to be found thereon.

Mr. President, I am convinced that this great effort, this great raid, which has been building up will reach its climax very soon. I believe that President Eisenhower will soon be under greater pressure to permit the raiding of natural resources than any other President has been put under for a generation. May God give him the wisdom and the strength to turn back the spoilers when they come to the White House seeking acquiescence in their plans. I hope the wee, small voice of conscience may speak to each and every member of Congress, reminding us of the sacred duty which we have to protect the heritage which properly belongs to our country and to posterity, and which has been entrusted to our keeping.

THE PRESIDING OFFICER: The Chair advises the Senator from Vermont that his time has expired.

MR. MURRAY: Mr. President, I yield an additional minute and a half to the Senator from Vermont.

MR. AIKEN: I thank the Senator.

The fourth question I ask myself is: Do we, by claiming ownership of the land under the salt water beyond the historic three-mile distance, and the right to dispose of this land, recognize the right of other countries to do the same? If we do, the effect of the passage of the pending joint resolution may result in closing great areas of the sea which previously have been open to international shipping, and eventually may involve us in controversies with other countries.

So, Mr. President, because I am unable to justify disposal of the undersea lands which from time immemorial have been held to belong to all the people of our forty-eight states, I shall vote No on the joint resolution.

PARTY POLITICS

THE FOUR FEARS [1]

ADLAI E. STEVENSON [2]

Mr. Adlai E. Stevenson gave this address at the Jefferson-Jackson Day Democratic dinner, Atlantic States Division, at Philadelphia, Pennsylvania, on Saturday, December 12, 1953. Some 1,400 attended the banquet in the ballroom of the Bellevue-Stratford Hotel, at $100 per head. The program was also broadcast over national radio and television networks (an ABC power break marred a few minutes of Stevenson's opening remarks).

Stevenson's attack on the record and policies of the GOP since their coming to power in 1953 suggested a preview of the issues and strategy to be stressed by the Democrats in the campaigns of 1954 and 1956. The speaker, recently returned from his trip around the world, had reported in talks and writings his reactions to our world relations.

At Philadelphia, Stevenson in effect endorsed Eisenhower's foreign policy. The President and the Democratic titular leader saw eye to eye on the atomic energy policy, the United Nations, the Korean armistice negotiations, the moves to strengthen NATO and to confer with the Soviets concerning Germany and Austria and peaceful relations in general. Whether the "right wing" of the Republicans would go along with such policy was another matter to be noted later.

The domestic scene, Stevenson emphasized, was a dark one—because of the machinations of such Republican thinkers and doers as McCarthy (not named) and Brownell (named). The activities of their dominant group, according to the speaker, "may please the Kremlin, but it will not build national unity or international respect. . . . Instead of the hope of the free world we have become its despair."

What were the results of these activities? We were beset with four fears—"fear of depression, of communism, of ourselves, and fear of freedom itself." The speaker gave the main body of his speech to threatened depression and the need to continue the stabilization of our economy according to the New Deal social and economic patterns. Here the speaker dealt with issues that would probably mark deep differences between the parties. For example, to what extent would the Republican legislation embody economic controls and the "further socialization" of

[1] Text and permission for this reprint supplied through the courtesy of Mr. Adlai E. Stevenson.

[2] For biographical note, see Appendix.

governmental tendencies? To what extent would the Republicans commit themselves to reciprocal trade agreements and to the gradual reduction of tariffs?

Stevenson at Philadelphia continued to reveal qualities in public address that distinguished him in the campaign of 1952. His philosophy was typically that of Roosevelt and Truman. His speech was free from clichés and banalities. His style was whimsical, sometimes sarcastic, but always dignified. He suggested a sense of the direction of history.

His voice was pleasantly keyed and resonant; it was well adapted to the radio, as was his presence to television. Although Stevenson at Philadelphia read, as he often does, he had a lively sense of communication. His pronunciation was that of family influence, European travel, and Eastern schooling—cultivated speech but still primarily "general American." [3]

Senator Myers, Mayor Clark, and Ladies and Gentlemen:

Hearing Alben Barkley speak here tonight reminded me that I was honored to second his nomination for Vice President here in Philadelphia in 1948. So I say to you that I proudly claim, in some measure at least, responsibility for the man whom we affectionately call the Veep.

I should like at the outset tonight to thank President Eisenhower for the initiative he has taken this week with respect to atomic materials and for his forthright reaffirmation of our desire for peaceful, friendly relations with the Russian people. And I also applaud the Secretary of State's emphatic rejection of recent assaults on our allies by Republican senators.

Speaking last September after a long journey I said there was grave anxiety about the world that the United States was inflexible; that we should be prepared to negotiate and should resume the initiative in the search for peace and disarmament. Some Republican leaders and editors promptly cried "appeasement."

I hope the President's words don't provoke similar epithets, because they are reassuring and will help to restore confidence in America's patience and peaceful purpose.

I am glad we are meeting in Philadelphia, which overflowed with brotherly love of a singularly Democratic variety at the

[3] For further comment on Stevenson as speaker, see *Representative American Speeches: 1951-52*, p 172-80; *1952-53*, p66-71, 83-91.

election last year while most of the country was seized with an uncontrollable fit of Republicanism. I shall never forget the comfort Philadelphia gave me on that not so enchanted evening. Indeed, I might actually have saved you all an hour's sleep and conceded an hour earlier had it not been for Philadelphia's resistance to the New Look of 1952—a fashion, by the way, which apparently is being rapidly discarded in many places.

Seeing Bob Meyner, the Governor-elect of New Jersey, reminds me that the New Jersey Republicans are still looking for the fellow who coined that phrase—"It's time for a change."

Measured by elections of late, our party's fortunes have suddenly improved, and it is well that we meet at year's end to appraise the comforting operating results of the past year, the condition of the company of Democrats and the opportunities and responsibilities ahead of us.

I am sure there are lessons for all of us in the Philadelphia story and a moral in the distinguished and forward looking leadership which Joe Clark, Dick Dilworth and their many able colleagues have brought to this great city—the lesson that good candidates, good organization and good government are the indispensable ingredients of political success nowadays.

And I am glad we are meeting here on the anniversary of Pennsylvania's admission to the Union, and in Philadelphia because in a special sense this is the home of American freedom. Here the Declaration of Independence was signed, and here the Liberty Bell rang out in Independence Hall. I have often wondered if my mother's Quaker ancestors heard it toll. It tolled for each of us, too—for the rights, the liberties, the dignities, and the duties, of every American citizen then, now and forever.

I know your hearts are troubled; the hearts of bewildered millions all across the earth are troubled, too, for the bell gives an uncertain sound in the confusing clamor of these times. The bill of rights is besieged, ancient liberties infringed, reckless words uttered, vigilante groups are formed, suspicion, mistrust and fear stalk the land, and political partisanship raises strange and ugly heads, the security of secret files is violated, and the specter of a political police emerges.

We begin to resemble the very thing we dread. The Attorney General, the chief law enforcement officer of the nation, the very embodiment of our concept of justice, has even imputed disloyalty or communist sympathy to a former President while our allies whom he organized, aided and armed to fight communism the world around listen in bewilderment and disgust.

As someone said, one wonders if those fellows will stop at nothing until they get Harry Truman out of the White House. And latterly some Republicans act as though they will stop at nothing till they get Dwight Eisenhower out of the White House, too.

But subversion and treachery are serious—and far more important than party politics. Doubtless there were mistakes, and there always will be, and they should be disclosed. But it is the facts which must be disclosed and not ugly distortions and insinuations.

Perhaps this clamor helps the Republicans politically but it will not solve the gigantic problems confronting us. The nation still has to be governed and a world defended. As I see it our duty as citizens first and Democrats second is not recrimination; it is not to defend or deny the past, for yesterday is irretrievable and the problems are now and tomorrow. What the Republicans do or don't do *now* is far more important than what the Democrats did or didn't do seven or eight years ago. Knocking each other out over the past may please the Kremlin but it will not build national unity or international respect. Fighting Democrats for political advantage is not fighting communism for national survival.

And we must never let unscrupulous politicians buy partisan advantage at the price of cherished liberties. Means are as important as ends. Fear is poison. And American influence cannot rest on money and military might alone, for principles are power—power in this world—the very power that distinguishes democratic freedom from Communist tyranny.

Thomas Jefferson wrote the Declaration of Independence in Philadelphia—and he went on to found the Democratic party, But the defense of individual liberty is the obligation—and the privilege—of all Americans. Today good Republicans stand with us in the conviction that no crisis can justify the impairment of our liberties—and in the determination that no enemy, abroad or at home, shall do so.

If the administration is looking for a good crusade I would recommend a crusade to combat the Commuinst conspiracy without resorting to Communist methods to do it.

They could get a lot of help from Democrats for that.

From the Bill of Rights to the Four Freedoms, we, Democrats, have tried to protect, to guarantee, and to enlarge the rights and liberties of the individual. From the dark days of the Alien and Sedition Laws to the present, we have fought those who had little faith in the people and who would control their thoughts, cramp and manacle their freedom. Resistance to tyranny has been our historic mission. Pray heaven it always will be and I have no doubt that *this* ugly alien mood of America, too, will pass away like others before it, and the Liberty Bell will ring again, deep-throated and clear, around this bewildered earth.

For these are the days of our strength in the world's peril. These should be the days of our greatness in the world's need. But instead of hope of the free world we could become its despair.

I believe that the President of the United States has set his face against all these things. But while he speaks of unity, his colleagues sow disunity. While he calls for calm, his friends light the fires of hysteria. While he invokes the American tradition that the accused has the right to be confronted by his accuser, members of his administration and his party charge, try, condemn and convict in a single action of the hand.

I only wish President Eisenhower could speak for the Eisenhower Administration. For, in the words of the Apostle, "If the trumpet gives an uncertain sound who shall prepare himself for the battle?"

It was only a few dozen years ago that a great American redefined and reaffirmed our heritage. I am speaking Franklin Roosevelt. I am speaking of the Four Freedoms—freedom of speech and expression; freedom of worship; freedom from want; freedom from fear.

Where are they today? Who speaks for them now?

Those gallant hopes of yesterday have given way to the sorry confusion of today. The Four Freedoms have been replaced by the Four Fears—fear of depression; fear of communism; fear of ourselves; fear of freedom itself.

And it is of the fear of depression that I want to say a word tonight, because, try as we may, we cannot escape the problems of today by taking refuge from the past.

Depression is a real fear for many of us. It has already touched the farmers. It may touch others in the months ahead.

Of course, there is a reason possibly for this fear. While there may be in some minds a relation between Republicanism and hard times, personally I don't believe in depression by association.

In all candor I don't know whether we are going to have economic misfortune or not. And I don't know for certain whether we can talk our way into a business recession. But I do know that talk alone won't prevent a depression or cure it either. The Republicans cleared up that question for us some twenty years ago.

As a Democrat I am proud that it was our party which first decided that unemployment for the worker, and bankruptcy for the businessman, and ruinous prices for the farmers, were not acts of nature; that economic misfortune was something free men in a free land could prevent; that with bold, decisive action Americans could master their own economic destiny.

Hence the disasters to American home and families of the past will not befall us with like severity again, thanks to social security, minimum wages, farm price supports, bank deposits insurance and control of dishonest securities and reckless speculation.

Home ownership has been made more secure. Farms are better financed. Income and taxes are more fairly distributed. Our forest, land and water resources have been protected and enlarged. In these and a dozen other ways, our economy has become more stable, more secure and more productive than ever before.

I call it a record of prudence and conservatism and I need not remind you that these steps to strengthen and stabilize our economy were nearly all taken over the vigorous opposition of the party now in power in Washington. They called us Socialists, but our works remain to lessen the chance that President Eisenhower and Secretary Humphrey will be afflicted by the same misfortune that befell President Hoover and Secretary Mellon. Sometimes I wonder whether our friends in Washington are adequately grateful.

What will it take to maintain economic stability? What is required of us? There are houses to be built and slums to be cleared. Our forests, public lands and parks need protection and improvement. We have watersheds to secure against the ravages of flood and erosion, and river valleys to develop. Roads, schools, hospitals are in arrears.

There is much more to vigorous anti-depression policy than public works. Any future downswing in economic activity must be the signal for a prompt readjustment of tax burdens to release money for private spending. And we should also expect, in the future, to make a more vigorous and courageous use of monetary policy than in the past. Farmers, businessmen, home owners and consumers must be assured of adequate credit.

We must also consider how improvements in our social security system and farm program can better our defenses against depression. When a worker loses a job, he is not the only one who suffers. The butcher, the baker, the grocer, all lose a customer; and the chain reaction runs through the entire economy. It is the same when the farmers' prices fall.

There are few better forms of insurance against economic misfortune than a sound farm program, and we all await with interest the new Republican farm program which has been so long in incubation—or should I say in commission?

Finally—and perhaps most important—we must give more emphasis to the part that business must play in a sound anti-depression program. Let us hope that we have seen the end of rancor and recrimination between business and government. In the future as in the past the vast majority of Americans must find employment on private payrolls.

Of late, we have heard some foolish talk from Washington about government for and by businessmen. Such talk is of no service to business. Most of us do not believe in government by any single interest, whether it be by industry, labor, farmers—or even the enlightened citizens of Philadelphia. And in the present climate of opinion there will be a strong temptation to turn all failures of the administration to the discredit of businessmen in general. Let us Democrats avoid this temptation. The task of building the security and prosperity of this land is a task for all. And, with intelligent and courageous leadership, confidence and common sense throughout the land, we need have no fear of the economic collapse Stalin so confidently and so often predicted.

If we have a depression in this country it will be man-made.

Prosperity in America is not our concern alone any longer. It is crucial to the world-wide restraint of communism and defense of freedom. An American depression would be the greatest gift we could bestow on the Kremlin. The architects of depression would be, in effect, the most successful Communist agents of them all.

This brings me to the subject of foreign trade, which is indispensable to the health and strength of the friendly world. Countries like Britain, Germany, Japan have to trade to live. They want trade, not aid, as much as we do.

But last year the dollar gap, the excess of our exports over our imports, was $5 billion. How can the gap be closed without giving them the dollars to buy our goods? How can other countries earn the dollars? There is only one way. If we are to sell our goods and surplus crops to other countries we must also buy their goods. We can also invest or loan dollars abroad which will help to balance the trade account and strengthen the economies.

They tell me that Pennsylvania under the shadow of Joe Grundy is not the place to discuss a more liberal trade policy. But our national well being demands that we prevent trade stagnation among the free countries.

It will be cheaper to import goods than export dollars.

It will make for a more stable economy here and abroad.

The continued prosperity of the farmer, the worker and the businessman depends to a large extent upon our export market.

Government help to injured industries and gradual tariff adjustments can prevent extreme hardship in most cases.

At all events, we shall have to make a choice between relatively minor adjustments caused by increased imports or major adjustments caused by decreased exports.

And, finally, we can be sure that if our friends and allies can't find markets and sources of supply outside the Iron Curtain, trade with the Communist orbit will grow. I doubt if anyone is going to starve to prove to us how anti-Communist they are.

We Democrats have a long, consistent record in favor of liberal trade policies since they first became a political issue. The nation can thank Cordell Hull, Franklin Roosevelt and a Democratic Congress for the Reciprocal Trade Agreements Act. Our party supported it almost unanimously and the Republicans opposed also almost unanimously. Many businessmen are coming abreast of our historic position. I hope the Republican party does, too.

It is a mistake to think only in defensive terms about economic policy as anywhere else. I would ask you to look ahead to our nation's future, not just in terms of depression, but in terms of growth; not in terms of disasters to be avoided, but goals to be achieved. With intelligence and will, we Americans have a reasonable chance of mastering our economic destiny. Using the best wisdom at our disposal, therefore, let us talk not just of avoiding setbacks, but of pressing ever forward on this unparalleled march toward abundance and strength in an expanding economy. For America has not ceased to grow—and will not so cease, until Americans as individuals falter in faith and nerve and cease to grow themselves.

I do not see our country huddled in a paralysis of fear—fearing foreign competition, fearing depression, fearing communism, fearing freedom, fearing ourselves. I do not see our country a

weathervane of anxiety, divided by bitterness and mean pursuits.
Rather I see it united in high endeavors, standing once again
before the world, calm, wise and resolute; a beacon of hope; a
citadel of fortitude—and of faith.

A long time ago, Benjamin Franklin, an old man then, cele-
brated for his hard, shrewd, common sense, stood here and said
to his quarreling countrymen: "The longer I live the more convincing proofs I see of this truth—that God governs in the
affairs of men."

Thank you.

PERSONAL TRIBUTE

ROBERT A. TAFT [1]

JOHN W. BRICKER [2]

Senator John W. Bricker (Republican, Ohio) gave this eulogy of Robert A. Taft, in the rotunda of the Capitol, on August 3, 1953, at the memorial services for the late Senator from Ohio. The Senator had died on the preceding Friday (July 31) in New York. On the day before the final Washington services the casket lay in state in the rotunda. Some thirty thousand passed the catafalque. Seating had been arranged for some nine hundred, including the Taft family, the Senate, Supreme Court, and President Eisenhower and his cabinet. There was a complete lack of ostentation. A marine orchestra played at the opening and close; Senate Chaplain Frederick Brown Harris gave the invocation, and House Chaplain Bernard Braskamp, the benediction.

Senator Bricker spoke in a low voice that "magnified and was endlessly distorted in the echoing cavern of the rotunda." His remarks, in keeping with the occasion, were highly personal, generous, but authentic as an analysis of Taft's leadership and personality.

Undoubtedly Taft was one of the five or six dominant speakers of his era. Vigorous in debate, unusually analytical in his understanding of domestic problems, he had the intense loyalty of millions of Republicans and the respect of most opponents. His three primary campaigns for nomination as the Republican candidate for the Presidency, and his fifteen years of active senatorial leadership demonstrated to the nation his abilities as thinker, stump speaker, able legislative debater, tireless committee room expounder and cross-examiner, and extempore radio discussant.

He was generally labeled as orthodox, an isolationist in succession to Henry Cabot Lodge, William E. Borah, and Hiram Johnson. He was unhappy about foreign entanglements, suspicious of Rooseveltian big government, "creeping socialism," "statism," and ill balanced budgets. Nevertheless, he supported United Nations participation and the Marshall Plan, but did so with many qualifications.

His forthrightness and mental independence were never absent. Often his bluntness cost him votes—but partly explained the final tributes to him and the titles of respect, "Mr. American," as well as "Mr. Republican." [3]

[1] *Congressional Record.* 99:11251-3, August 3, 1953 (daily edition)

[2] For biographical note, see Appendix.

[3] For a considerable list of Taft's speeches, with comment by this editor, consult the Index to this volume.

The heart of our nation is heavy today. Its head is bowed. A grateful people are saddened by the death of their faithful servant, Robert A. Taft. In the words of Edwin Markham:

> And when he fell in whirlwind, he went down
> As when a kingly cedar—green with boughs—
> Goes down with a great shout upon the hills
> And leaves a lonesome space against the sky.

In him were personified the noblest attributes of the Republic —reverence of God and love of liberty.

He was my closest political friend. Countless others could call him such. He gathered to himself loyal friends in every walk of life.

Humble in victory, without rancor in defeat he traveled far along life's road to great achievement. Service to others is the toll we pay as we travel life's highway. For every mile along his way, he paid in devoted service to his fellow man.

There are many roads in life which one may follow. Some lead to quicksands of tyranny, and some to freedom. Some roads lead to individual despair and others to happiness. Many roads lead to destinations unknown. Senator Taft was always ready to use his legislative influence to erect a helpful sign for the benefit of his fellow citizens traveling along life's many highways and byways. He never hesitated to recommend the coercion of law to prevent the stronger travelers from impeding the progress of the weak. He used his voice and his vote to help those stranded in the march of life through no fault of their own. His consistent political creed, however, was that the power of government should not be used to make the individual march on any particular road. Bob Taft left that choice to the individual just as it was left to him and to us by our forebears.

He was clear of thought and blunt in speech but sincere conviction rang in every word. As Lincoln said of Henry Clay:

> His eloquence did not consist, as many fine specimens of eloquence do, of types and figures, elegant arrangement of words and sentences, but rather of that deeply earnest and impassioned tone and manner which can proceed only from great sincerity and thorough conviction in the speaker of the justice of his cause. He never spoke merely to be heard.

Greed for power never goaded him. There was no scheming and no conniving in his makeup. Bob Taft would not compromise with wrong nor waver on a principle. He did not run with demagogues.

A great man of God in a Senate prayer said—as we well remember—"O Lord, give us men with a mandate higher than the ballot box." That prayer was answered in Senator Taft. He seemed touched with a quality which came from beyond the greed, the pettiness, the passing passions of the hour.

From an early age Robert Taft seemed destined for leadership. Grandson of a Secretary of War and Attorney General of the United States; son of a President and Chief Justice of the United States, he adorned a great family record.

In his mother's memoirs we read of his grandparents:

Judge Alfonso and Mrs. Taft had created a family atmosphere in which the children breathed in the highest ideals, and were stimulated to sustained and strenuous intellectual and moral effort in order to conform to family standards. They had an abiding confidence in the future of their children which strongly influenced the latter to justify it.

Through three generations of this family, the same could well be written. Bob Taft had a great pride in the four fine sons he and his beloved Martha have brought to manhood and success.

The day when Senator Taft last appeared on the Senate floor, I sat next to him and asked him how he was feeling. He answered: "I feel better because I spent the weekend at home with my family and didn't have to go to the hospital." To him, Martha and his family were first in his love and affection. His family carries on a great heritage.

Bob Taft stood first in his class at Yale when he received his baccalaureate degree, first in his class at Harvard when he took his law degree, and attained highest honors in the bar examination in Ohio. He was a leader of our bar, a truly great lawyer, associated in many of the most important cases of the past thirty-five years.

But it was in political life that his leadership was to reach its zenith. He was speaker of the Ohio House of Representatives, leader in the Ohio Senate, and in 1938 with his election to the United States Senate, opportunity for national leadership opened wide to him. Truly, the United States Senate was his field.

In 1944 he came to my home and told me he would be a candidate for reelection and then told me his great desire was to be a real leader in the United States Senate. We today are comforted that he so nobly achieved that innermost yearning.

Senator Taft was a true liberal, as a review of his record will show and as people more and more realize. He believed in the most freedom possible for the individual consistent with orderly society. In the cataclysm of two world wars, individual freedom threatened to become submerged in the power of government. But through it all Senator Taft stanchly kept the faith that was his. He knew that finally the principle of human liberty must prevail.

Like Thomas Jefferson he waged an unrelenting war on all forms of tyranny over the minds of men. He championed unpopular causes and espoused unorthodox views regardless of political consequences. He insisted on the same right for others. In exercising the right of every American to challenge the validity of all doctrines and of all beliefs, he was nevertheless aware of a profound political paradox—that some things are beyond challenge. One does not challenge the value of freedom; one does not question that mankind has inherent God-given rights; one does not doubt the value of the American Constitution to secure those rights; one does not doubt that those rights are divinely bestowed. All this is a matter of political and religious faith, without which no political leader, whatever his talents, can be called great in the American tradition. The American system, as he so well knew, is truly builded upon a spiritual foundation. In Senator Taft's memory new leaders will arise, inspired by his devotion, to carry the torch of true liberalism toward the final goal.

Senator Robert A. Taft's whole life was one of deep convictions, of confidence in the ultimate victory of right and righteousness. When convinced of the rightness of a cause, he stood firm even though he stood alone.

Examples of his unflinching courage could be cited endlessly. In 1946 a transportation strike was paralyzing America. Public sentiment overwhelmingly favored drastic action. Both the President and the House of Representatives recommended conscription of striking workers. The Senate seemed likely to follow. It was due primarily to Senator Taft that this precedent for tyranny was not established. Though he stood virtually alone at first, his action soon received nation-wide acclaim. This was only one case out of many justifying his confidence that the truth as he saw it would ultimately prevail.

Senator Taft was a man of great faith. He had faith in himself born of a great intellect, indefatigable industry and manifold experiences. He had faith in his fellow man. That faith in others led them to put their trust in him.

He had a great faith in our kind of government. His life was dedicated to its preservation and its betterment. His compass was the Constitution of his country; his ultimate goal—a better life for his fellow man. To paraphrase Emerson—governments have their development in the moral identity and character of men.

This stricken leader had a great vision of the meaning of government. It was not for the few, not for the strong, but for the individual, for the good of all that government should be organized. He believed truly in his heart that all men are created equal.

More important than all these things, Bob Taft had a deep and an abiding faith in Almighty God. He was an active churchman and to him the organized church was God's way of lifting up the lives of people.

He had a true faith that there is a divine providence working in the hearts and souls of men guiding us toward a day of better understanding, nobler relationships and peace on earth, good will among men, for which the Master whom he worshipped came and lived and gave his life. He believed there is a life hereafter in the spirit world. Those of us who have the faith to believe as he did know that his noble spirit lives on, for "In the way of righteousness is life; and in the pathway thereof there is no death." [Proverbs 12: 28.]

One of the imperishable yearnings of the soul of man is to live beyond the day of death. During life, our departed leader created to himself an everlasting memorial. His services to his government and through government to his fellow man will go on and on. Many hereafter, because of his ennobling example, will gain inspiration to serve in the cause to which he gave his full devotion. That will be our lasting memorial in his honor.

A grateful nation bestows its sympathy to his loved ones in this hour of their bereavement.

May the Father of us all strengthen and sustain them.

No more fitting words can be found than those penned by the immortal Tennyson:

> On God and godlike men we build our trust.
> He is gone who seemed so great—
> Gone, but nothing can bereave him of the force
>   he made his own
> Being here, and we believe him
> Something far advanced in state,
> And that he wears a truer crown
> Than any wreath that man can weave him.
> Speak no more of his renown,
> Lay your earthly fancies down,
> And in the vast cathedral leave him,
> God accept him, Christ receive him.

BENJAMIN FRANKLIN [4]

HERBERT HOOVER [5]

Former President Herbert Hoover, chairman of the Commission on the Reorganization of Government, gave this short address upon receipt of the Gold Medal of the International Benjamin Franklin Society, New York City, on January 23, 1954.

Edward R. Murrow, in introducing Mr. Hoover by film on his television program, "See It Now," on January 26, said: "Someone said that you can always get the truth from a man who is past seventy and who has given up all hope of being President. The other day the International Benjamin Franklin Society awarded Mr. Hoover a gold medal, and in accepting it, he reminisced a little bit about the 'great man' and added a few comments of his own."

Mr. Hoover here appears in lighter vein and with a mellowness of voice and personality noticeable in his later days. Millions continue to hold him in highest respect as statesman, citizen, and as platform or dinner speaker.[6]

I deeply appreciate the honor of receiving the gold medal from the International Benjamin Franklin Society.

I am presumed to say something about Franklin, but how can I add anything new to what has been said about him? The members of your Society ought to know all about him by this time.

The rest of the country has also heard of him. With appropriate remarks his name has been fixed to thousands of counties, towns, cities, and streets. Millions of parents have striven to implant his qualities of character in their offspring by endowing them with the surname of Franklin. That includes two Presidents. One result is that his name appears in five thousand telephone directories. To carry a conviction of integrity a thousand firms have labeled their goods after him. There is one library alone of ten thousand items about him. There must have been twenty million orations delivered about him.

---

[4] Text furnished through the courtesy of Mr. Herbert Hoover, with permission for this reprint.

[5] For biographical note, see Appendix.

[6] For further comment on Mr. Hoover as speaker and for examples of his speeches, consult the Index of this volume.

Some members of your committee suggested that I should say something about Franklin's influence on American life at the present time. I investigated this subject a little but I came up (on all but one great issue) with many frustrations, as I will proceed to show you.

My first acquaintance with Franklin began early when, like most schoolboys of my day, I received much drilling in Franklin's precepts. They at times seriously limited my freedom of action and my projected enterprises. Especially objectionable was his remark about early to bed and its consequences in health, wealth and wisdom provided we got up early in the morning.

Aside from human liberty, Ben's great design of American life or his ideology, as we would call it nowadays, had its central idea in frugality, thrift and hard work. He conducted a propaganda campaign on that subject for over sixty years. His slogans sunk so deep into the American mind that we practiced at it for quite a while. However, that was before we discovered the theory of spending ourselves into prosperity.

Franklin had definite ideas on the conduct of governments. His opinion of governmental borrowing and debts appear in his abundant command of the language. To him they were the road of sorrow and in general the destroyers of liberty. He knew none of the joys provided by Lord Maynard Keynes. However, this is not an economic debate and I believe it better not to pursue that subject further at this time.

Franklin also made some observations on money. He asserted that "The standard once fixed should ever be unvariable since any alteration would be followed by great confusion and detriment to the state." He was naturally unfamiliar with the theory and practice in the commodity dollar. But again that subject leads into a field of controversy not appropriate here.

Ben also observed that "It is impossible for government to . . . fix the extent of paper credit," and also that "no state or potentate can settle the prices of all sorts of merchandise [because] . . . plenty and scarcity must govern that." But this again raises questions which might be construed as controversial and must, therefore, not be pursued further at this time.

As to the industrial front he stated firmly that "God gives all things to industry," meaning hard work, and he intimated that you could save what you earned. But some people these days think the government takes it away from you and then gives it away. However, this would also be a sour theme to pursue on this occasion.

Franklin made one remark that is of powerful weight today. He said that "God helps those who help themselves." That has become the motto of every pressure group in the country. But I will not pursue this pessimistic subject at this time.

Franklin had many notions of government. Using the architectural metaphor, he once said, "If the superstructure is too heavy for the foundations the building totters though assisted by outward props of art." I suppose the props of art he referred to was propaganda. He would have been even more forcible on this subject if he were in my place as Chairman of the Commission on Reorganization of the Government.

Franklin announced a formula for public office. He said, "Never ask, never refuse, never resign." The present Administration in Washington has found the "never resign" part is still in use.

But again I must not pursue such subjects here. I did think something might be done by way of comment on Franklin's fine stimulation to investigation and research. This seemed promising as the magnificent educational and research institutions which he founded have been fruitful of blessings down to this very day. But among institutions that he had a lot to do with creating was the United States Senate. Their spirit of education and investigation would seem rewarding to him, but perhaps also that theme is not profitable on this occasion.

Ben always referred to himself as a Republican but certainly in this nonpartisan meeting I cannot pursue this idea further.

On all controversial matters Franklin was a tolerant soul. He cautioned us that "By the collision of different sentiments, sparks of truth are struck out and political light is obtained." I hope so. But I will not illustrate it further.

He said, "It is true that in some of the states there are parties and discords; but let us look back and ask if we were without them. Such will exist wherever there is liberty; and perhaps they will help preserve it." I call your attention to the safety catch in that sentence—that is the use of the word "perhaps."

Ben made the emphatic remark that "they that can give up essential liberty to obtain a little temporary safety deserve neither liberty nor safety." Some way I feel Ben might be disappointed with the world on this subject. Indeed I have the feeling that staunch old emblem in his plain clothes with his radiating thrift would receive many shocks if he walked around on this earth for a few days. However, with his magnificent sense of humor, he might just laugh.

But to be more serious, we know the greatest inheritance that Franklin left the American people was his contribution to our liberties.

Franklin had sought and associated with men keen in devotion to freedom long before we gained our independence from England. Among his friends were Burke and Tom Paine. It is sometimes overlooked that it was Franklin who paid Tom Paine's shipfare across the Atlantic and set that firebrand of liberty on these shores. It was Tom Paine, then a soldier in the Continental army, who as a ghost writer for Washington composed that blazing document which Washington proclaimed to his dejected troops, revitalizing them to the victorious crossing of the Delaware. And Tom Paine with his crusading spirit and his "Rights of Man," greatly stirred the emotions for personal liberty on this Continent.

I scarcely need mention, however, that Franklin was one of the leaders among the Founding Fathers who riveted freedom into American life. We must never forget that Franklin helped frame and signed the Declaration of Independence. He negotiated the peace Treaty of Paris, acknowledging our freedom from Britain. He contributed greatly to the framing of the Constitution of the United States. And in those great deeds he was inspired by both genius and determination to guarantee national independence and to secure the very foundations of personal liberty.

Franklin was an individualist. He held no belief in people's leaning on government. He contended they must have a sterner fare if the nation was to go forward. He insisted they must possess qualities and strength of character which would give them calmness and poise in prosperity and courage and vision in adversity. They must be guided not only by patriotism of the tribe, but by morality and religious faith which belong alone to the individual spirit.

It was Joseph Choate who said, "When the spirit of Franklin decays the sun of America will have begun to set."

NATIONAL IDEALS

FREE INVESTIGATION AND FAITHFUL EXPERIMENT [1]

EARL WARREN [2]

Chief Justice of the United States Earl Warren gave this address at the annual Alexander Hamilton dinner of the Association of the Alumni of Columbia College, Columbia University, at the Waldorf-Astoria Hotel, New York City, on the evening of January 14, 1954.

More than 1,600 persons were present. The Chief Justice's address was carried, coast to coast, by the Columbia, National, American, and Mutual Broadcasting networks. Federal Judge Harold Medina presided. Other speakers included President Grayson Kirk of Columbia University.

This occasion was part of the University's bicentennial celebration. The theme was "Man's Right to Knowledge and the Free Use Thereof." The year's program included three academic convocations: the first was held on January 11; the second was scheduled for June 1, and the third, October 31. Numerous other conferences were scheduled, many of them broadcast to the nation. Chief Justice Warren's address, his first major one since he was sworn in on October 5, centered upon his proposition that a free world is to be realized entirely by the free nations who have a monopoly on the concepts and practices of freedom.

Chief Justice Warren is not a master of "great eloquence." His effectiveness lies more in his content (as illustrated in this speech). His language, in this address, is here and there strikingly original. The sentence length and complexity would seriously limit the appreciation of the speech by "mass" audiences.

The Chief Justice's voice lacks resonance and is monotonous. He is seldom if ever impassioned. His robust personal appearance, his bodily animation, his attitude of friendliness, good will, and statesmanlike integrity give him strong ethical appeal and compensate for lack of superior oratorical manner.[3]

[1] Text furnished by Columbia University, and permission for this reprint through the courtesy of Columbia University and Chief Justice Earl Warren.

[2] For biographical note, see Appendix.

[3] For further comment on Chief Justice Warren as speaker, see article by W. Charles Redding, of the University of Southern California, in "Political Speaking in 1952—A Symposium," edited by A. Craig Baird, in *Quarterly Journal of Speech*, 38:279-84, October 1952.

Mr. Toastmaster, President Kirk, distinguished visitors from the educational centers of the world, and friends of Columbia University:

I rejoice with all of you at being able to share in the celebration of such an important birthday of an institution that has contributed so greatly throughout American history to our institutions, our culture, and generally to our national life. I believe implicitly in the worthwhileness of such celebrations, not as an opportunity for self-glorification but primarily for introspection; as a tribute to those generations of worthy and hardy souls who, as scholars and teachers throughout the free world, have hitched civilization to the stars, and who, perhaps more than any other group, have been responsible for the leavening influences in society and for the advances made in the tortuous climb to the good life by people everywhere. They also give us the opportunity to inventory our assets and liabilities, to more clearly define the road we have traveled and to make more certain the direction in which we are headed. Particularly is this important in a chaotic world where even the most fundamental values are being questioned, and where the propaganda of fierce ideologies arouse the counter toxins of fear, hatred and at times even imitation.

These celebrations afford those of us who are in the welter of our changing world to say a word of appreciation to those who devote their lives quietly, with little regard and less opportunity for adequate monetary compensation, to the pursuit of unadulterated truth in the halls of our educational institutions and in the laboratories of our great foundations for the advancement of mankind. They are entitled to such public recognition from what I believe is a grateful American citizenry.

This is the two hundredth birthday of Columbia University. By the measuring rod of eternity, a period of two hundred years is but a grain of sand; measured by the civilizations of the past or even the older cultures of today, it is not great; but measured by the life of our great nation—a nation that itself is not that old and that did not even have self-government two hundred years ago, it is indeed a long time. Measured in relation to present day civilization, which has brought into the lives of people the telephone, the electric light, the automobile, mechanical perfection, the airplane, radio, television, radar, wonder drugs and atomic energy—all of them within the lives of people still living—it is both a long and important span of time.

Measured in relation to the advances made in the social sciences and in the opportunity for self-government in every quarter of the globe, it is a thrilling period of time.

And how fitting it is that this great university should adopt for the theme and spirit of this celebration on its two hundredth birthday the words "Man's Right to Knowledge and the Free Use Thereof." It is appropriate first because it represents what always has been the spirit of this university and through which it has made such great contributions both to our institutions and to our way of life and, secondly, because through man's right to knowledge and the free use thereof, we find our greatest possibility for an ultimately free world in which man need not fear his neighbors on either side of political boundary lines and where knowledge acquired and exchanged can be used for the betterment of human kind everywhere. And if such an existence is to be achieved, we of the free world must accomplish the result by ourselves. The field is left entirely open to us. We have an absolute monopoly in it. No Communist government, no Fascist government, no government that is totalitarian could tolerate that approach to the problems of life. It would not tolerate institutions in which such a spirit abided, because the teachers and students, uninhibited in their pursuit of ideas, would soon generate ideas that would cause the totalitarian state to crumble. Such governments can not tolerate dissenting views. All must bow to one creed, one party, one faith. There is no room for diversity, no room for free play of the mind, no allowance for the dictates of conscience.

That is why the oppressive shackles which communism places on people will be—must be—ultimately thrown off. Liberty— not communism—is the most contagious force in the world. It will permeate the Iron Curtain. It will eventually abide everywhere. For no people of any race will long remain slaves. Our strength is in our diversity. Our power is in freedom of thought and of research. When men are free to explore all avenues of thought, no matter what prejudices may be aroused, there is a healthy climate in the nation. Dissenters can let off steam. That is important, too. The greatest figures in American history have always recognized this as inherent in our system. The founding fathers themselves were not orthodox either in thought or expression. They recognized both the right and the value of dissent in their generation.

In one of the first law lectures given by James Kent in 1794 at Columbia College, he said:

> I am most thoroughly, most deeply persuaded that we are favored with the best Political Institutions, take them for all in all, of any People that ever were united in the Bonds of Civil Society. The goodness of these Institutions will brighten on free investigation, and faithful experiment, and be respected according as they are understood.

"Free investigation" and "faithful experiment" were the ideals of the greatest Justices of our Supreme Court—Marshall, Holmes, Brandeis, Cardozo, Hughes, and Stone.

"Free investigation" and "faithful experiment" were the guiding principles of Washington, Jefferson, Lincoln, and our other great Presidents, including the one whom this University recently gave to our country—Dwight D. Eisenhower.

These men did not merely mouth these sentiments; they believed them; they acted in accordance with them. They breathed them into our institutions. In their endeavor to make freedom secure and permanent throughout the land, all recognized that our universities and colleges must be the places where the false and the evil can be segregated from the good by the processes of free discussion and free inquiry. They were all patrons of education and recognized that the more turbulent the times the more essential the freedom of inquiry. We are now living in such times. Our universities and our colleges are, therefore, even more precious to us now than in normal times. To preserve the true spirit of these institutions we must recognize that "free investigation" and "faithful experiment" are essential if society is not to become stagnant or is not to store up the seeds of its own destruction.

It was my privilege for almost eleven years, because of my position as Governor of California, to sit on the Board of Regents of its University, my own alma mater. I believe in no other way could I have become so well acquainted with its importance in the life of our state, nor in the problems of higher education in America. My university is also a great university. It too attracts students from distant parts of the world, but its greatness comes largely from the fact that it has learned much through the years from older universities, like your own, as younger and smaller colleges are now benefiting from its manifold activities. In composite, all these institutions, hundreds of them throughout the nation—young, old, large, small, wealthy, poor, public, private—are the leaven in the loaf of our national life. In their friendly and free competition—not to be larger or wealthier— but to serve better, they inspire our youth and infuse into our social, economic and political life the tensile strength essential to progress and national unity.

From this vantage point, I learned first hand some of the budgetary problems of higher education, the pressures to contract curricula to so-called "practical subjects," the failure to recognize growth and the blanket criticisms sometimes made of educators. I also saw from a distance the problems of dwindling endowments for so many private colleges and universities. In the aggregate, these problems weigh heavily on our educational system which in the main has accomplished so much for our country in such a comparatively short period of time.

Everyone should understand these problems, and I am sure it would not be inappropriate for the citizens of every community to gather in school buildings, city halls and court houses as you are gathered here for serious and even prayerful discussion of the subject of this Bicentennial Celebration—"Man's Right to Knowledge and the Free Use Thereof."

I know my associates on the Supreme Court of the United States would have me extend their greetings to the officers, faculty, students and friends of Columbia University, and express their appreciation for the services renedred by its graduates and scholars to the constitutional system which we are dedicated to support and strengthen. We do not forget that the War of the Revolution interrupted the studies here of Alexander Hamilton who did as much to secure the ratification of our Constitution and to implement it as any other American. We do not forget Gouverneur Morris of your Class of 1768, who with him and your then President, William Samuel Johnson, were in the Constitutional Convention and signed the immortal document for New York, Connecticut and Pennsylvania. Nor do we forget that on numerous occasions throughout our history, Columbia graduates have filled the most important governmental posts in the nation.

But the fact that is most significant to us is the part Columbia men have played on the Court itself. Throughout the years, it has contributed members for it. My associates of today, William O. Douglas and Stanley F. Reed, received their inspiration for the law here on Morningside Heights. Since the Court was first organized in 1789, Columbia's contribution of justices, attorneys general, solicitors general, judges and members of the bar have contributed mightily to the body of constitutional law which guides our actions and secures our freedom. I would like to mention three of them—the three Chief Justices that Columbia has contributed among the fourteen who have held that office—John Jay of your Class of 1764, Charles Evans Hughes of the Law Class of 1884, and Harlan Fiske Stone of the Class of 1898.

John Jay was the first Chief Justice of the United States, and in his brief tenure made a contribution which is today part of the very texture of our government. He and his associates established the principle that the judiciary is independent of the executive, and decides only actual cases and controversies. George Washington, as President, had requested the advice of the Court on various questions of law arising out of French and British treaties. Jay's court declined to give any advisory opinion on the questions. That restriction on the Court's function, once and for all, established the Court as a purely judicial body.

Chief Justice Hughes and Chief Justice Stone had long tenures on the Supreme Court, and the contributions they made will be enduring. Both of these men knew law from life as well as the books. Both had a wide, practical experience in the law and in public administration. They brought to their judicial offices wisdom, practical judgment and a sense of the purpose and continuity of law. To say that, however, is not enough. For these men were statesmen as well as lawyers. They realized that orderly change was as important as stability; that the law could not be a living thing serving the needs of every oncoming generation if it should always be anchored to the status quo and to preconceptions of the past. And, they were not always on the popular side. That is often the case where judges and public officials protect freedom of speech, of the press and of assembly as they did.

In *Stromberg* v. *California,* 283 U. S. 359, 369, Chief Justice Hughes wrote:

The maintenance of the opportunity for free political discussion to the end that government may be responsive to the will of the people and that changes may be obtained by lawful means, an opportunity essential to the security of the Republic, is a fundamental principle of our constitutional system.

Again in *De Jonge* v. *Oregon,* 299 U S. 353, 365, he wrote:

The greater the importance of safeguarding the community from incitements to the overthrow of our institutions by force and violence, the more imperative is the need to preserve inviolate the constitutional rights of free speech, free press and free assembly in order to maintain the opportunity for free political discussion, to the end that government may be responsive to the will of the people, and that changes, if desired, may be made by peaceful means.

The instances could be multiplied. Certain it is that the record of Chief Justice Hughes on these fundamental issues is a valiant one. He, as much as any judicial officer in our history, caught the spirit of our free institutions and realized the importance to society of tolerance for the multitude of views, ideas, and tastes that people have. He saw that the strength of our system was in the diversities which it allows. He saw long before totalitarianism became a living world menace that there was grave danger to our institutions in any effort to force the minds of men into any one political, philosophical or religious mold.

Chief Justice Stone, who sat as an Associate Justice from 1925 to 1941, and as Chief Justice from 1941 to 1946, served in the same tradition. He was usually with Hughes in such decisions while they were together on the bench. It was he who wrote:

The sober second thought of the community is the firm base on which all law must ultimately rest.

Both Stone and Hughes knew that the "sober second thought" of the American community after people had an opportunity for "free investigation and faithful experiment," was always for freedom for the mind and the conscience.

And Chief Justice Stone lived to see the "sober second thought" of the Supreme Court itself adopt, for its decisions, his dissenting opinions of a former day.

These men were indeed stalwart sons of your great university. Almost two hundred years after it came into being, they were still strengthening the spirit of that provision of its original charter which provided that the college should not

exclude any person of any religious denomination whatever from equal liberty and advantages, on account of his particular tenets in religion.

It is impossible of calculation and perhaps even of imagination to appraise the accomplishments of the thousands of graduates of Columbia University who have been infused into the life of the nation, but we do know that they are to be found in every part of America and in every walk of life. We know also that many of them have left a definite personal imprint on our culture, our economy and our government. In the aggregate, they have been a potent factor in the development of a nation of 160 million people; people of every racial origin, of every cultural background, of every governmental experience, and, therefore, of every conceivable viewpoint and approach to our problems; people who have nonetheless built a nation wherein they can agree upon the fundamentals of life and government and abide by them under a Constitution that is of their own creation and subject always to their own will. I like to believe that this has been made possible by merging many viewpoints rather than conforming to one, and that even at this date "the goodness of these institutions will brighten on free investigation and faithful experiment" as was truthfully said at Columbia in 1794, when both your university and our nation were planting the seeds of their greatness. I congratulate you on the advances you have made. I share your aspiration and your belief that traveling in the same direction, Columbia University is destined for other centuries of even greater progress.

ARE WE WORTH SAVING? [4]

ELMER DAVIS [5]

Mr. Elmer Davis gave this Phi Beta Kappa oration at Harvard University on June 8, 1953. The speaker's issue was, Are we worth saving? If so, why and how? The answer of this oration was, "What we have to offer is a method; and the freedom of mind that makes that method possible."

If the earlier sections of the address were historical and formal, the thought progress was clear and provided a solid basis for later specific propositions. It was a semi-inductive approach to the constructiveness of the final paragraphs. There Davis focused on concrete treatment of the "primitives" that would stifle this "freedom of mind." His conclusion: "Be strong and quit yourselves like men; and fight."

Impressive were the historical analysis in this address (Davis is a former Rhodes Scholar, well grounded in history and philosophy); the formality, clarity, and originality of phrasing; the whimsical astuteness that cropped up—a frequent accompaniment of Davis' radio and television broadcasts.

Davis' pronunciation is Midwestern, his tones flat, and his inflections emphatically conversational with little trace of the rhythms of formal oratory. Yet his vocal expression often conveys the emotional and imaginative reaction of genuine eloquence. This warmth of delivery, together with his forthrightness of statement, was an important explanation of his popularity. After 1939 he had millions of listeners on the Columbia Broadcasting System and later on the American Broadcasting Company networks.[6]

A century or so ago a Harvard graduate wrote a hymn whose opening line, plausible enough when written, turned out to be one of the most inaccurate forecasts ever set down:

The morning light is breaking, the darkness disappears.

[4] The text is from *Harper's Magazine*, 207:23-30, August 1953. Permission for this reprint through the courtesy of Elmer Davis and through special arrangement with him and the Author's League of America, Miss Luise Sillcox, Secetary.

[5] For biographical note, see Appendix.

[6] For further comment on Davis as speaker, see *Representative American Speeches: 1939-40*, p63-7, "Finland Surrenders"; *1941-42*, p 111-18, "If We're Good Enough We Can Take It." For Learned Hand's address, referred to by Davis, see *Representative American Speeches: 1952-53*, p121-9.

The final couplet of that stanza, however, would—with the omission of a single word—be a fairly accurate picture of the world today:

> Each breeze that sweeps the ocean brings tidings from afar
> Of nations in commotion, prepared for Zion's war.

Commotion indeed; but it is not Zion's war for which they are preparing. Yet in his day the Reverend Samuel F. Smith seemed to have good reason for his confidence in the success of the missionary enterprises that were then spreading over the world; and not only in their direct success but in the derivative benefits that would flow from them. He had faith—not only faith in his religion; but back of that, like most men of his day, he had the general confidence of the Western world in that golden afternoon; the immensely successful nineteenth century; an assurance that it had not only a religion but a culture which was so good in itself that it was the Christian duty of all who possessed it to extend it to less favored races.

To its intended beneficiaries that assurance must often have seemed arrogance. Especially as expressed in the most famous missionary hymn of the time—

> By many an ancient river, from many a palmy plain,
> They call us to deliver their souls from error's chain.

The call was audible mostly to the inner ear, but there it rang loudly.

> Shall we whose souls are lighted by wisdom from on high,
> Shall we to men benighted the lamp of life deny?

Responding to that appeal, many men and women went forth into the foreign field, performed the most heroic, arduous, and often hazardous labors, and sometimes laid down their lives. We owe them the utmost respect; yet I am sure we all wish that the appeal had been phrased more tactfully. The missionary techniques of Olaf Trygvasson no longer commend themselves; but at least, when he gave his subjects the choice between accepting the lamp of life and getting their throats cut, he didn't pretend that they had asked for it.

But Bishop Heber and the Reverend Samuel Smith profoundly believed what they wrote, as did most men of their time. The principal group that disagreed with them, the Hardshell Baptists, did so only in an even greater faith—that when God chose to save the heathen He could do it by Himself, without the help of contributors to foreign missions. Logically and theologically they seem to have had the better of the argument; but they were a feeble and dwindling group because the vast majority was inspired, for the most part unconsciously, by a faith which comprehended and transcended theology. The great Protestant missionary effort of the nineteenth century, like the great Catholic missionary effort of the sixteenth century, was the expression of a strong and vigorous culture—different phases only of the culture of what we call the Western world, through a Polynesian or even a Japanese might reasonably ask, West of what? In the sixteenth century the West was just awakening, with a delighted surprise, to an awareness of its own strength, which had seemed gravely in question in the opening phases of the Turkish onslaught. By the nineteenth century the West had no doubt that it was the culmination of all human progress to date, with even more dazzling achievements lying beyond.

In the middle of the twentieth century the principal questions in dispute among Western intellectuals seem to be whether the West can be saved, and if it is worth saving. The two most popular of recent historical philosophers both think the Western world is going down hill, and one of them seems to feel that it won't be much loss. Spengler appreciated the loss more than Toynbee; if he felt that it was inevitable, that was perhaps because he was an artist rather than a philosopher. Yet, though it may be only a coincidence, it is certainly a disquieting one that he and Toynbee, starting from very different premises, come out to about the same conclusion as to the phase of development that our civilization has reached; and still more disquieting, as to what lies ahead—what Spengler called Caesarism, and Toynbee the universal state.

There are optimists of course who think that a really universal state—a world-wide state—could be created by some other means than military force; Spengler and Toynbee are not among them nor, to compare small things with great, am I. So long as Communists remain Communists any world coalition government would be subject to the same dangers, and likely to meet the same fate, as the coalition governments of Poland and Czechoslovakia; and there is still wisdom enough in the West not to run that risk. Others think that even if a universal state were created by military force, the result would not be Caesarism—provided of course that our side won. A couple of years ago Bertrand Russell was one of these; lately he seems to have become discouraged, and offers us the variant but not very cheerful prospect of a dual Caesarism, with Premier Malenkov and President McCarthy dividing the world between them, and collaborating to suppress dissent in both their realms. I do not suppose that Russell was entirely serious in suggesting this; he may only have been reading Orwell's *1984,* or he may have been reading the *Congressional Record.* Such a future seems improbable; but in the world we live in, no one can be sure that it is impossible.

Spengler is dead and can write no more; he has said his say; within his artistic scheme, the progressive deterioration of any culture seemed inevitable. Any man who keeps on writing and talking is likely to contradict himself; Toynbee has written so much that he has involved himself in about as many contradictions as Dr. John H. Watson, when he set down the history of Sherlock Holmes. A few years ago Toynbee seemed to have some hope that the creative minority of our civilization had not yet lost its creativity, not yet become a merely dominant minority, for the inadequacy of whose rule the internal proletariat would have to compensate by creating or adopting a universal religion; now he seems to think we have passed the point of no return. We passed it, apparently—or at least so he thought when he delivered the Reith Lectures last year; he may since have changed his mind again—we passed it toward the end of the seventeenth century, when men became disgusted with the endless religious wars which neither side ever decisively won, and turned to secular interests—turned from preoccupation with preparation for the next world to consideration of what could be done with this one; and, increasingly, to what could be done with it through technology.

And for this apostasy, thinks Toynbee, God has punished us—punished the West by the loss of the East; not only our territorial possessions and our commerce there but our moral influence in an East which increasingly turns toward our Communist enemy. The East rejected our religion, and our technology with it, when they were parts of an indivisible way of life; it accepted our technology when it was divorced from our religion (and incidentally had become far more efficient, that is to say far more worth accepting) with consequences which became apparent at Pearl Harbor in 1941 and more recently in Korea. "The fortunes," he says, "of Western civilization in the mission field veered right around from conspicuous failures to conspicuous successes as soon as its attitude toward its own ancestral religion had veered around from a warm devotion to a cool skepticism." Which appears to mean, when the mission field had become the field of a new kind of missionary, offering no longer the lamp of life but oil for the lamps of China, and all that went with it.

History does not support this interpretation. It has lately been subjected to a number of searching criticisms—notably by Professor Michael Karpovitch in the *New Leader* and by G. F. Hudson in *Commentary*. Karpovitch, after pointing out that Toynbee is wrong on all the things that Karpovitch knows most about, suavely admits that no doubt he is right in other fields. Hudson makes a more general attack on the entire doctrine, to which a layman can offer only a couple of corroborative footnotes. The great success of Protestant missions—not to mention a vigorous revival of Catholic missions, and the beginnings of the penetration of the East by Western technology as well—came at a time when the cool skepticism of the eighteenth century had been buried under a new wave of evangelical fervor; when Protestantism was not only as vigorous but as dogmatic as the Catholicism of the Counter-Reformation. (I do not know whether Toynbee regards Modernist Protestantism as a religion at all; but he can hardly deny that title to Fundamentalist Protestantism.)

What at present appears to be the failure of Protestantism in China seems to be due less to divine wrath at apostasy than to an intensified form of the thing that caused the eventual failure of Catholicism in Japan, when it had lost little if any of its energy and fervor in Europe—the fear of a suspicious and despotic government that religion had been merely the cover for imperialistic political intrigues. In either case there was little evidence on which to base that fear; but despots need little evidence—especially despots newly come to power, who still feel insecure.

It might indeed be argued that the West, in its relation with the East, is being punished for its sins; but the sin is not apostasy, it is too great faith. The sin that is most surely and sharply punished is a mistake—however well intended, however it may have seemed at the time the thing to do. The punishment is often delayed, and falls on the descendants of those who made the mistake; often on innocent bystanders. "Those eighteen upon whom the tower of Siloam fell, and slew them—think ye that they were sinners above all men that dwelt in Jerusalem?" We are authoritatively assured that they were not; the sin was that of the architect or the contractor, the punishment fell on people who only happened to be around. Many Europeans and Americans have suffered in Asia, and may presently suffer in Africa, for mistakes for which they were in no way responsible—mistakes made from the highest motives, as a result of faith.

For alongside the theological religion of the West, which in the past two and a half centuries has had its ups as well as its downs, there was growing up in Western Europe and America a secular religion, held as fervently by devout Christians as by rationalists—the faith in freedom, in self-government, in democracy. (Indeed the only living ex-President of Columbia University has more than once implied that only believers in a theological religion can believe in this secular religion too. The evidence for this cannot be found in history.) The Westerners who interpenetrated the East in the nineteenth century, whether missionaries, engineers, business men, or administrators, mostly carried this religion with them. They made many mistakes; but it was devotion to this secular religion that led them to make what, from the standpoint of practical consequences, was the worst mistake the West ever made in dealing with the East. They educated the natives.

Not merely in the operation of modern weapons, for the greater convenience of Western powers warring among themselves; these were men of faith, faith in the whole Western culture of which this secular religion was becoming steadily a more important part. Many of those whom they educated sprang from cultures far older than ours, and in some respects more distinguished; but it was the Western culture that seemed to work; so it did not have to be forced on them; in this case they really did call us to deliver their minds, at least, from error's chain. We educated them in Western medicine and engineering, in Western government and law. And in the course of that education the pupils were exposed to the fact that there were such things as freedom and self-government and democracy—things which the educators obviously regarded as good for themselves; it was only a question of time till the pupils began to suspect that they might be good for everybody. Educate any man, of whatever race or color, in what he didn't know before and you are taking a chance; how he will turn out will depend somewhat on the education but more on his background and environment and on what was in him to start with; you may get a Nehru and you may get a Jomo Kenyyatta. The one thing they have in common is a conviction that those who educated them, having fulfilled that function, ought to get out.

I have enough faith in that secular religion to believe that in the long run the consequences of this will be beneficial—as they seem to be already in the successor states of the Indian Empire. But that is no consolation to those on whom various towers of Siloam have fallen elsewhere.

This digression was necessitated by the fact that the most popular of contemporary historians has offered an explanation not only for our unsatisfactory relations with Asia and Africa, but for the general dilemma of our times—an explanation which not only to me but to many of my betters seems no explanation at all. But what then is the matter with us? What have we left, if anything, that is worth saving?

This first and obvious answer, of course, is, "If we aren't worth saving, who is?" Faulty as we are, we seem infinitely preferable—by our standards—to the moral nihilism and intellectual rigidity of the Soviet system which is competing with us for the allegiance of the East; competing indeed, though with little success outside of France and Italy, for the allegiance of our own citizens. Unfortunately, we do not always seem preferable to those among whom our missionaries, and those of the opposition, are working; and if through force or deception they have once accepted the opposition's gospel they find that the choice is irrevocable. Rebels on the barricades would be blown to pieces by tanks and bombing planes; indeed the secret police would never let anybody get to the barricades in the first place.

G. F. Hudson—following Orwell—holds that modern totalitarian techniques would make impossible even Toynbee's last refuge for the disconsolate, wheresoe'er they languish—the creation by the internal proletariat of a universal church to compensate for the shortcomings of a universal state. "If Nero," says Hudson, "had had the resources of the MVD at his disposal, the early Christians would have been publicly confessing how in their vileness they had set fire to Rome on instructions of the King of Parthia." In the world we live in, freedom once lost is lost to stay lost. We had better remember that, in dealing with our internal even more than with our external problems.

Granted however that from anything that could be called an ethical viewpoint we are better worth saving than our adversaries, this is no proof that we are going to be saved unless we have the qualities that enable us to save ourselves. Faulty as was the western Roman Empire, it was far more worth saving than the barbarian tribal dominions that surrounded it and eventually overran it; but its own faults brought it down. This is worth mentioning since not only Spengler and Toynbee, but lesser men, have dealt with our predicament in terms of what befell civilizations of the past; and these analyses, however embellished with facts, or conjectures, from Chinese and Mayan and Sumerian history, all rest pretty much on the one case about which we have tolerably complete information—the decline and fall of the Roman Empire. Many historians have attempted to explain it; almost all of them, even Gibbon—even Rostovtzeff—seem to me to explain it largely in terms of their own experience, and observation of their own times.

I shall not add to that confusion, but shall only point out one or two details in which our situation is different. We know now that the happiness and prosperity of the age of the Antonines, which so impressed Gibbon, was only relative; considerable no doubt compared to what had gone before and what was to come afterward; but behind the splendid front there was a dry rot inside. Economically the Empire was deteriorating, and intellectually too.

Economically the Western world is doing pretty well nowadays; and in the English-speaking and Scandinavian countries the problem that Rome never solved and that finally did more than anything else to bring Rome down has been solved with a fair degree of success—the problem of passing prosperity around, of seeing that everybody gets some of it. If France and Italy solved that problem too, the Communist parties in those countries would soon shrink to the hard core. Our civilization, says Rostovtzeff—lately echoed and emphasized by Professor Robinson of Brown—our civilization will not last unless it be a civilization not of one class but of the masses. This is a warning that might more pertinently be directed toward the Soviet Union than the United States, in so far as what exists in the Soviet Union can be called a civilization. As for Rostovtzeff's last despairing question, "Is not every civilization bound to decay as soon as it penetrates the masses?" we can only say that we shall in due course find out. We have started in that direction and we can't turn back.

The Romans, outside of the cities, never got started; and even there civilization was a narrowing pyramid, with a hollow top. The most notable thing about the age of the Antonines was its intellectual sterility, in a period of rest betwen calamities when the Western world might have made vast advances, and fortified itself against the calamities that were to come; the classic case of what Toynbee calls the loss of creativity in the dominant minority. Are we losing it? Dr. J. G. de Beus of the Netherlands Embassy in Washington, who has lately analyzed these forecasts of the future, thinks the Western world is still vigorously creative—not only in science and technology, but in politics, domestic and foreign; and in art and letters as well.

It is perhaps fortunate that this optimistic view was set down before the recent sculptural competition in London for a statue of the Unknown Political Prisoner, where the prize was given to a contraption in wire that looked like nothing, unless perhaps a television aerial. As for letters, most of the most admired literature of the Western nations—especially the English-sepaking nations—for thirty-five years past has been to all appearance the effluvium of a sick society. English literature, between wars, gave us an almost unrelieved picture of a nation in process of dissolution from its own internal weakness—a nation that would collapse in ruins as soon as somebody pushed. But the time came when somebody pushed, and it did not collapse; indeed the people who did the pushing eventually did the collapsing too.

Many American novelists have written about the late war. Most of their works would be intelligible if written by Frenchmen after 1870, or Spaniards after 1898—mercilessly candid pictures of the inner decay that led to calamitous defeat. But since we happened to win the war, something seems to have been wrong with the picture—not no doubt with the individual picture which each man saw; but with the total picture which few of them ever noticed.

This phenomenon is a symptom of what has been called the alienation of intellectuals from the life around them, which is taken very seriously by intellectuals. I cannot see that it makes much difference. The intellectuals wrote their books, which often sold widely; the society around them bought the books, read them, and ignored them. Indeed their authors usually ignored them when the chips were down; men who had spent their lives proving that the United States was not worth fighting for went out and fought for it like everybody else.

The first condition of the survival of any civilization is that it should win its wars. Rome did, till its armies wore themselves out fighting one another. I think that from the military point of view we could win the next war, if we should have to fight it, despite the weakness of our air defense in the northeastern approaches. But to win a war under modern conditions requires more than military strength—more even than preservation of a sound dollar. It requires political shrewdness, domestic and foreign, to a degree the Romans seldom had to practice. For five centuries after the battle of Magnesia they had virtually no need for a foreign policy, till the degenerate days when they found it necessary to make an alliance with one German tribe against another. The United States, as the *prima inter pares* of a coalition, has to deal with complexities convincingly set forth not long ago by the President, who has had more experience in dealing with coalitions than any other man since Metternich. It would not be easy to cope with them, even if he had the actual (though not the theoretical) power of a Roman Emperor; it is not so easy in a republic whose Constitution, as Woodrow Wilson once put it, permits the President to be as big a man as he can. If he cannot be or does not want to be a big man, there will be plenty of others who will volunteer to fill the vacancy.

What a civilization like ours which is not a universal state, but a coalition of independent powers, can do to insure its own continuance depends quite as much on how each state manages its own internal affairs. Here the Romans met the proximate cause of their disaster. When they had a good man at the head of the state all went well—unless he was a good man like Antoninus Pius; perhaps the most virtuous of all rulers of a great realm and certainly pre-eminent in manly beauty; but he appears to have been only a glorified Calvin Coolidge, who sat there and went through the motions while the problems piled up for his unhappy successor. But when the Romans got a bad man in, there was no way to get him out except by assassination or revolution. Over a period of ninety years almost every Emperor —and they were many—was got out by one or the other of those methods—good men as well as bad.

The nations which embody Western civilization are no longer subject to that danger, but their political systems have other defects. Mr. Walter Lippmann remarks that if the free world is in peril, it is not because our enemies are so strong, but because the free nations are so badly governed; and they are badly governed because of the usurpation of power by the national legislatures. . . . Well—we must discriminate. In the nations of the British Commonwealth the supremacy of the legislature is the essence of their constitutions, and they have learned how to make it work. In the French Republic it is also the essence of the constitution; in the three-quarters of a century of the Third and Fourth Republics they have not learned how to make it work. In our own republic it is in flat conflict with the Constitution, and no wonder it doesn't work. It is an old story; long before the present publicized attacks on the State Department, and on the President's control of foreign policy, the principal problem of our government was congressional usurpation, usually through committees, of executive functions. Congress not only tells administrators what they must do, which is its right; but how to do it, which is not its right, and is wholly outside Congress's field of practical competence as well as of authority.

A Congress which ate raw meat during the last few years of a Democratic Administration has shown that it is not going back to a milk diet just because the Republicans are in power. Nor would it do so even in wartime unless compelled, as it has been compelled by every strong President. Until the question whether it would be so compelled again may arise, we might reflect that all the periods of congressional government in our history have been periods either of bad government or of do-nothing government. There have been times when we could afford a do-nothing government; we can afford it no longer. Still less a bad government.

But to return from this digression into the factors that will make it practically possible—or practically impossible—to save us; back to the original question, Why should we be saved? What have we got that our adversaries have not that makes us worth saving? Our faults, God knows, are numerous and glaring enough; recognition of those faults is the chief cause of the loss of confidence that has afflicted so many people of the Western world. But we do recognize them; we do not pretend that our failures were decreed by ineluctable historical necessity; nor do we rewrite history according to the precepts of Double-think, to prove that they never happened at all.

What we have to offer, to the contemporary world and to the future, is a method; and the freedom of the mind that makes that method possible. Not an infallible method, but the best yet discovered for reaching increasingly closer approximations to the truth. It will never offer its conclusions with such assurance as does dialectical materialism—which, by a singular coincidence, always seems to produce the conclusions that are convenient for the men in power. It can only say, We have kept the door open for exploration of all possibilities, consideration of all objections, application of all possible tests; and this is what seems to be true. Maybe something else will seem more probable later on, but this is the best we can do now. Or, as the method was summarized long ago—Prove all things; hold fast that which is good.

This method has been responsible for almost all human progress. Outside the Western world it does not exist, except in those parts of the East which have been influenced by Western thought; if it died here, it would die there too. President Conant has remarked that the right to think and question and investigate is the basic difference between the free world and the world of totalitarianism. It might well be the basic difference that would save us, if it came to a shooting war; and whether it does that or not, this one thing—the scientific method, and above all the freedom of the mind that makes it possible—is what makes us worth saving. As G. F. Hudson has observed, "To repudiate faith in freedom is to abandon Western civilization."

The founders of this Republic held that faith so firmly that its guarantee was embedded in the very first amendment to the Constitution—almost a part of the original document. Yet lately that faith has been repudiated by many of our fellow-citizens, if indeed they ever held it; and in that repudiation lies our greatest danger; it is this, rather than any external attack, that might bring us down. That repudiation takes various forms, and appears on various levels. One phase of it was the recent attack on the Bureau of Standards and particularly the manner in which the Secretary of Commerce questioned its objectivity. As Eugene Rabinowitch lately wrote in the *Bulletin of the Atomic Scientists*, the government has the right, if it should so choose, to subordinate the findings of science to the demands of business; but it has no

right to attempt to coerce the scientists into adjusting their findings to those demands. That is Lysenkoism; it is something we
had better leave to the enemy.

But far more widespread and more dangerous is the general
attack on the freedom of the mind. George Kennan said at
Notre Dame that it springs from forces too diffuse to be described
by their association with the name of any one man or any one
political concept; forces which perhaps were summarized by John
Duncan Miller of the London *Times*, in the early days of Mc-
Carthyism, as a revolt of the primitives against intelligence.
Unfortunately it cannot be denied that after centuries of education
we still have plenty of primitives—some of them white-collar or
even top-hat primitives; a sediment, a sludge, at the bottom of
American society—and I am afraid a fairly deep layer at that;
people who seem actuated only by hatred and fear and envy.
All the products of ignorance; for their fear is not a rational fear
of a very formidable and unfriendly foreign power; I have
received thousands of letters from people like that in recent
years and they do not seem interestd in Russia at all. They appear
to regard communism as a purely American phenomenon; what
they hate and fear is their own neighbors who try to think. In
the name of anti-communism they try to strike down the freedom
of the mind, which above all things differentiates us from the
Communists; in the name of Americanism they try to suppress
the right to think what you like and say what you think, in the
evident conviction—in so far as they have any reasoned conviction at all—that the principles on which this Republic was
founded and has been operated will not bear examination.

That of course is not true; but if we do not stand up and
resist the people who feel that way, this movement toward sup-
pression will be successful. It is people who feel that way who
provide the mass support for McCarthy; though of course he has
an elite support as well, if it may be so termed, in the reactionary
press and the Texas oil billionaires. He has already done serious
injury to the United States government—especially to the State
Department, on which we must chiefly rely for avoidance of war;
and he has done more than any other man to encourage the

spread of suspicion and distrust and hatred among ourselves, which is the best formula for losing a war.

We have now reached the point where, if agents of the FBI appear in the home town of a prominent man and begin asking questions about him, his neighbors know that he is either on his way to jail or is destined to appointment to high office in the United States government. I doubt if such confusion is healthy. I venture to remind you of the remark by Judge Learned Hand, in a speech so often quoted that perhaps you all know it by heart; nevertheless I remnd you that he said he believe that that community is already in process of dissolution where each man begins to eye his neighbor as a possible enemy, where non-conformity with the accepted creed is a mark of disaffection; where denunciation takes the place of evidence and orthodoxy chokes freedom of dissent.

If we are not to become such a community, the friends of freedom will have to stand up and fight.

Some men who have sentimental predilections in favor of freedom lack the guts to fight. The State Department ran out on the appointment of Mildred McAfee Horton because it was afraid of a fight in the Senate. (This is not a conjecture or an inference; it is a fact.) The Department offered the charitable explanation that this would have been very unpleasant for Mrs. Horton. She didn't seem afraid of it at all; but it would certainly have been unpleasant for the State Department, which weeps with delight when McCarthy gives it a smile, and trembles with fear at his frown.

For the last few minutes I have been talking, not about Western civilization, but about the United States. And without apology, for we are the principal component of Western civilization, at least in the material sense; if we go down it all goes down—and when we confront a totalitarian dictatorship, whatever goes down stays down; it doesn't get up again. And we shall go down, unless we recognize what we have to fight for, and have the courage to fight for it. What makes Western civilization worth saving is the freedom of the mind, now under heavy attack from the primitives—including some university graduates—who have persisted among us. If we have not the courage to defend that faith, it won't matter much whether we are saved or not.

I do not think Stalin could have licked us; I do not think Malenkov and Molotov, Beria and Bulganin, can lick us. But McCarthy and the spirit of McCarthyism could lick us—no doubt without intention, but they could; by getting us to fighting among ourselves like the Romans, by persuading every man that he must keep on looking over his shoulder, to make sure that the man beside him doesn't stab him in the back. There is still enough vitality in Western civilization to save us, unless we insist on disemboweling ourselves.

I should perhaps have begun this sermon with a text, a text taken from the fourth chapter of the first book of Samuel, the eighth and ninth verses—the mutual exhortations of the Philistines before the battle of Ebenezer. "Woe unto us!" they said, when they realized that the Israelites had brought the Ark of God with them to battle. "Woe unto us! Who shall deliver us out of the hands of these mighty gods?" But then, realizing that nobody else was going to deliver them, they said to one another, "Be strong, and quit yourselves like men; and fight." And they did fight, and delivered themselves. So may we; but only if we quit ourselves like men. This republic was not established by cowards; and cowards will not preserve it.

CONSTITUTIONAL CHANGES

FOR SEGREGATION IN THE SCHOOLS [1]

JOHN W. DAVIS [2]

John W. Davis delivered this plea before the United States Supreme Court, on December 7, 1953, to uphold separate schools for Negroes and whites.

The final oral arguments were on this occasion presented in five cases in which the right of Kansas, South Carolina, Virginia, the District of Columbia, and Delaware, to segregate Negroes and whites in the public schools was challenged. Davis, "dean of American constitutional lawyers," represented South Carolina. Each lawyer, interpreting the briefs previously presented to the Justices, was limited to one hour. Eleven hours in all were taken up by the arguments. The courtroom, seating three hundred, was crowded.

The case, appealed from the District Court decision upholding the legality of segregation, concerned itself with the issue, Should the principle of "separate, but equal" education in the schools (that is, segregation) be abolished? The question was one of the most momentous to confront the Supreme Court. More specifically, was the intent of the Fourteenth Amendment to include prohibition of segregation in the schools? Did that amendment imply that Negroes were to be raised to "complete equality" with the whites? Related issues, suggested by the Court itself, and answered by Davis, were: Has the Court power to interpret the amendment so as to prohibit such segregation? If so, should the Court issue decrees to bring about a gradual change to mixed schools? Or should lower courts issue such decrees?

The opposing point of view was ably presented by Thurgood Marshall, of New York, counsel for the National Association for the Advancement of Colored People.[3]

On May 17, 1954, the Supreme Court ruled unanimously that segregation of Negro and white students in public schools is unconstitutional.

[1] The text is from *The State,* Columbia, South Carolina, December 12, 1953. The reprint was made possible through the cooperation and courtesy of John W. Davis. Because of the length of the argument, only the statements on chief issues are here reprinted.

[2] For biographical note, see Appendix.

[3] For Mr. Marshall's argument, see p 118-21.

Davis' entire argument was an admirable forensic. The issues were clearly set forth and answered with completeness and with ample citation of evidence. The essential refutation was inserted at appropriate points. The ethical components were skillfully incorporated with dignified treatment of opponents, courtesy but not undue deference toward the judges, and with no trace of arrogance in the unfolding of the arguments. As the speaker progressed he became more personal and emotional, and the address ended with an appeal, somewhat reserved, but not unlike Webster's conclusion in the Dartmouth College case, in which Webster (according to Chauncey Goodrich) declared that "It is a small college, but there are those that love it," and moved Chief Justice Marshall to tears. Mr. Davis, as he argued this case of segregation, "choked up and was visibly affected by emotion," according to Richard Wilson, Washington correspondent for the Des Moines *Register* (issue of December 8, 1953).

Davis, facing the nine justices, spread before him the record on appeal, and the various briefs. With a few notes only, he extemporized with complete ease and yet with aptness of language. His voice was still sonorous. He who had addressed his countrymen as presidential candidate in 1924, who had argued more than 140 cases before the higher court, who had responded on many occasions for speeches of anniversary, dedication, or law association gatherings, still retained before the Supreme Court, in this his eightieth year, much of his earlier eloquence.

May it please the Court, I suppose there are few invitations less welcome in an advocate's life than to be asked to reargue a case on which he has once spent himself, and that is particularly unwelcome when the order for reargument gives him no indication whatever of the subjects in which the Court may be interested, and, therefore, I want to at the outset tender the Court my thanks and, I think, the thanks of my colleagues on both sides of the desk for the guidance they have given us by the series of questions which they asked us to devote our attention to, and in what I shall have to say, I hope to indicate the answers which, for our part, we give to each one of them. . . .

We have in South Carolina a case, as Mr. Marshall has so positively admitted, with no remaining question of inequality at all, and the naked question is whether a separation of the races in the primary and secondary schools, which are the subject of this particular case, is of itself per se a violation of the Fourteenth Amendment.

Now, turning to our answers, let me state what we say to each one of them. The first question was: What evidence is there that the Congress which submitted to the state legislatures and conventions which ratified the Fourteenth Amendment contemplated or did not contemplate, understood or did not understand that it would abolish segregation in public schools?"

We answer, the overwhelming preponderance of the evidence demonstrates that the Congress which submitted, and the state legislatures which ratified, the Fourteenth Amendment did not contemplate and did not understand that it would abolish segregation in public schools, and in the time that is afforded, I hope to vindicate that categorical reply. . . .

The question with which Your Honors are confronted is: Is segregation in schools a denial of equality, where the segregation runs against one race as well as against the other, and where in the eye of law no difference between the educational facilities of the two classes can be discerned? . . .

The second question: If neither the Congress, in submitting, nor the states, in ratifying, the Fourteenth Amendment understood that compliance with it would require the immediate abolition of segregation in public schools, was it nevertheless the understanding of the framers of the Amendment (a) that future Congresses might, in the exercise of their power under Section 5 of the Amendment, abolish segregation or (b), that it would be within the judicial power in light of future conditions to construe the Amendment as abolishing such segregation of its own force?

And to that we answer it was not the understanding of the framers of the Amendment that future Congresses might, in the exercise of their power under Section 5 of the Amendment, abolish segregation in public schools, and, (b) it was not the understanding of the framers of the Amendment that it would be within the judicial power, in light of future conditions, to construe the Amendment as abolishing segregation in public schools of its own force. . . .

The third question: On the assumption the answers to questions 2 (a) and (b) do not dispose of the issue: Is it within the judicial powers in construing the Amendment to abolish segregation in the public schools? And we answer it is not within the judicial power to construe the Fourteenth Amendment adversely to the understanding of its framers as abolishing segregation in the public schools.

Now, I want to spend some time on the fourth and fifth questions. They give us little disturbance, and I don't feel they will greatly disturb the Court.

As to the question of the right of the Court to postpone the remedy, we think that adheres in every court of equity, and there has been no question about it as to power.

The fifth question, whether the Court should formulate a decree, we find nothing here on which this Court could formulate a decree, nor do we think the Court below has any power to formulate a decree, reciting in what manner these schools are to be alternative at all, and what course the state of South Carolina shall take concerning it.

Your Honors do not sit, and cannot sit as a glorified Board of Education for the state of South Carolina or any other state. Neither can the District Court.

Assuming, the language of the old treaties about war, it is not to be expected and that God forbid, that the Court should find that the Statutes of the State of South Carolina violated the Constitution, it can so declare.

If it should find that inequality is being practiced in the schools, it can enjoin its continuance. Neither this Court nor any other court, I respectfully submit, can sit in the chairs of the legislature of South Carolina and mold its educational system, and if it is found to be in its present form unacceptable, the State of South Carolina must devise the alternative. It establishes the schools, it pays the funds, and it has the sole power to educate its citizens.

What they would do under these circumstances, I don't know. I do know, if the testimony is to be believed, that the result would not be pleasing.

Let me say this for the state of South Carolina. It does not come here as Thad Stevens would have wished in sackcloth and ashes. It believes that its legislation is not offensive to the Constitution of the United States.

It is confident of its good faith and intention to produce equality for all of its children of whatever race or color. It is convinced that the happiness, the progress and the welfare of these children is best promoted in segregated schools, and it thinks it a thousand pities that by this controversy there should be urged the return to an experiment which gives no more promise of success today than when it was written into their Constitution during what I call the tragic era.

I am reminded—and I hope it won't be treated as a reflection on anybody—of Aesop's fable of the dog and the meat: The dog, with a fine piece of meat in his mouth crossed a bridge and saw the shadow in the stream and plunged for it and lost both substance and shadow.

Here is equal education, not promised, not prophesied, but present. Shall it be thrown away on some fancied question of racial prestige?

It is not my part to offer advice to the appellants and their supporters or sympathizers, and certainly not to the learned counsel. No doubt they think what they propose is best, and I do not challenge their sincerity in any particular period but I entreat them to remember the age-old motto that the best is often the enemy of the good.

AGAINST SEGREGATION IN THE SCHOOLS [4]

THURGOOD MARSHALL [5]

Thurgood Marshall, Negro counsel for the National Association for the Advancement of Colored People, delivered this argument before the United States Supreme Court on December 8, 1953. He was the leading speaker for abolition of segregation in the schools, against John W. Davis, for segregation.[6]

Four questions were submitted by the Court to those arguing the case: (1) Did the framers of the fourteenth amendment intend it to prohibit segregation in the schools? (2) Has the Court the power to interpret the amendment that way? (3) If so, should it issue decrees to bring about a gradual abandonment of segregation? (4) Or should the lower courts issue such decrees?

The two-day presentation before the Supreme Court opened on December 7, with Spottswood W. Robinson III and Thurgood Marshall, for the appellants, followed by John W. Davis and his associates for the appellees. On the next day, Marshall refuted the argument of Davis of the previous day. On May 17, 1954, the Supreme Court ruled unanimously that segregation of Negro and white students in public schools is unconstitutional.

Marshall has had a distinguished career as constitutional lawyer. His voice is deep and resonant. His forensic manner is calm, dignified, direct, but with occasional intense emotional vigor. He advises young lawyers: "Lose your head, lose your case."

His arguments of December 7 and 8 were frequently interrupted by questions from the Supreme Court justices. Marshall has demonstrated much extempore skill in such colloquies and a full revelation of mastery of fact and inference.

This case before the Supreme Court was one of the most historic in that court's long history. Students of argumentation, public address, political science, and history are advised to analyze in detail the entire case.

A part of Marshall's extended refutation of Davis' argument is printed below.

---

[4] This reprint is through the courtesy and cooperation of Mr. Thurgood Marshall. The text is from the transcript of the arguments on the segregation issue, as delivered on December 7-8, 1953. The complete two-day argument was recorded by Ward and Paul, 1760 Pennsylvania Avenue, N.W., Washington, D.C.

[5] For biographical note, see Appendix.

[6] For details of the occasion see the Introduction to John W. Davis' "For Segregation in the Schools," p 113-17.

It follows that with education, this Court has made segregation and inequality equivalent concepts.   They have equal rating, equal footing, and if segregation thus necessarily imports inequality, it makes no great difference whether we say that the Negro is wronged because he is segregated, or that he is wronged because he received unequal treatment. . . .

And finally I would like to say that each lawyer on the other side has made it clear as to what the position of the state was on this, and it would be all right possibly but for the fact that this is so crucial.   There is no way you can repay lost school years.

These children in these cases are guaranteed by the states some twelve years of education in varying degrees, and this idea, if I understand it, to leave it to the states until they work it out—and I think that is a most ingenious argument—you leave it to the states, they say, and then they say that the states haven't done anything about it in a hundred years, so for that reason this Court doesn't touch it.

The argument of judicial restraint has no application in this case.   There is a relationship between federal and state, but there is no corollary or relationship as to the Fourteenth Amendment.

The duty of enforcing, the duty of following the Fourteenth Amendment, is placed upon the states.   The duty of enforcing the Fourteenth Amendment is placed upon this Court, and the argument that they make over and over again to my mind is the same type of argument they charge us with making, the same argument Charles Sumner made.   Possibly so.

And we hereby charge them with making the same argument that was made before the Civil War, the same argument that was made during the period between the ratification of the Fourteenth Amendment and the *Plessy* v. *Ferguson* case.

And I think it makes no progress for us to find out who made what argument.   It is our position that whether or not you base this case solely on the intent of Congress or whether you base it on the logical extension of the doctrine as set forth in the McLaurin case, on either basis the same conclusion is required, which is that this Court makes it clear to all of these states that in administering their governmental functions, at least those that are vital not to the life of the state alone, not to the country alone, but vital to the world in general, that little pet feelings of race, little pet feelings of custom—I got the feeling on hearing the discussion yesterday that when you put a white child in a school with a whole lot of colored children, the child would fall apart or something. Everybody knows that is not true.

Those same kids in Virginia and South Carolina—and I have seen them do it—they play in the streets together, they play on their farms together, they go down the road together, they separate to go to school, they come out of school and play ball together. They have to be separated in school.

There is some magic to it. You can have them voting together, you can have them not restricted because of law in the houses they live in. You can have them going to the same state university and the same college, but if they go to elementary and high school, the world will fall apart. And it is the exact same argument that has been made to this Court over and over again, and we submit that when they charge us with making a legislative argument, it is in truth they who are making the legislative argument.

They can't take race out of this case. From the day this case was filed until this moment, nobody has in any form or fashion, despite the fact I made it clear in the opening argument that I was relying on it, done anything to distinguish this statute from the Black Codes, which they must admit, because nobody can dispute, say anything anybody wants to say, one way or the other, the Fourteenth Amendment was intended to deprive the states of power to enforce Black Codes or anything else like it.

We charge that they are Black Codes. They obviously are Black Codes if you read them. They haven't denied that they are Black Codes, so if the Court wants to very narrowly decide this case, they can decide it on that point.

So whichever way it is done, the only way that this Court can decide this case in opposition to our position, is that there must be some reason which gives the state the right to make a classification that they can make in regard to nothing else in regard to Negroes, and we submit the only way to arrive at that decision is to find that for some reason Negroes are inferior to all other human beings.

Nobody will stand in the Court and urge that, and in order to arrive at the decision that they want us to arrive at, there would have to be some recognition of a reason why of all of the multitudinous groups of people in this country you have to single out Negroes and give them this separate treatment.

It can't be because of slavery in the past, because there are very few groups in this country that haven't had slavery some place back in history of their groups. It can't be color because there are Negroes as white as the drifted snow, with blue eyes, and they are just as segregated as the colored man.

The only thing can be is an inherent determination that the people who were formerly in slavery, regardless of anything else, shall be kept as near that stage as is possible, and now is the time, we submit, that this Court should make it clear that that is not what our Constitution stands for.

Thank you, sir.

FOR THE BRICKER AMENDMENT [7]

Hugh Butler [8]

The late Senator Hugh Butler (Republican, of Nebraska), spoke over radio station KRVN, Lexington, Nebraska, addressing himself especially to his Nebraska constituency, on January 10, 1954. At that time the Senate of the Eighty-third Congress, second session, began prolonged debate on the Bricker amendment to the Constitution.

Senator Bricker's proposal would change fundamentally the constitutional provisions for dealing with international treaties and the conduct of foreign policy. Under the amendment no treaty could take effect unless Congress passed additional legislation "which would be valid in the absence of the treaty." Thus the change would prevent any treaty's overriding an individual state's power. Another provision would limit the President's authority to conduct foreign affairs and to enter into agreements with foreign governments without congressional concurrence. (This provision, section 3 of the amendment, provoked immense controversy.) Senator Butler simplified for popular understanding this difficult constitutional problem.

Many business leaders, lawyers, farmers, veterans, and isolationist groups strongly supported the Bricker point of view. President Eisenhower, internationalists, supporters of the United Nations, some law associations, and "liberal" thinkers argued against the change.

On Friday, February 26, the original Bricker amendment and the various substitute or compromise amendments were defeated, 60 to 31—one vote less than the two-thirds required for the passage of a proposed constitutional amendment. The final vote was not on the Bricker resolution nor on the original substitute proposed by Senator William F. Knowland (Republican, California), but on one put forth by Senator Walter F. George (Democrat, Georgia).

The closeness of the final vote and the complexity of debate in the legislative development indicated that the issue was by no means dead.[9]

Fellow Nebraskans, this is your Senator, Hugh Butler, bringing you once again my regular monthly report on important national policies and problems that I think will be of interest to you.

[7] Text supplied through the courtesy of Senator Butler, with his permission for this reprint.

[8] For biographical note, see Appendix.

[9] For Senator Butler's political leadership in recent years, see *Current Biography: 1950.*

Today I am going to devote most of my time talking to you about the so-called Bricker amendment which is one of the more important items to be considered by Congress this session.

The Bricker amendment, which is actually Senate Joint Resolution No. 1, was introduced in the Senate last January by Senator Bricker and sixty-two other senators, including myself. This resolution is popularly known as the Bricker amendment because Mr. Bricker's name appears first on the resolution, and also because it is a proposed amendment to the United States Constitution. The purpose of the Bricker amendment is to change the United States Constitution to protect American rights and the American form of government against the dangers of treaty law. The amendment provides for three things:

Section 1: That no provision of a treaty which conflicts with the Constitution of the United States shall be of any force or effect;

Section 2: A treaty shall be effective as internal law in the United States only through legislation which would be valid in the absence of a treaty.

Section 3: Congress shall have the power to regulate executive agreements and such agreements shall be subject to the same limitations as treaties.

At this point, you may be interested in the history of treaty law, and just why this amendment is so vital to the welfare of our country.

The Constitution of the United States operates as a guide for all laws made in this country. This simply means that a law passed by any legislative body which contradicts any portion of our Constitution is absolutely null and void. The Supreme Court of the United States is the highest court that decides this question. Whenever a law is passed by Congress, a state legislature, or any other legislative body that takes away the protection afforded by the Constitution, we always see such law challenged in the courts where it is declared to be unconstitutional; or in other words, to have no effect whatsoever. You may wonder why it is now necessary to amend the Constitution in order to maintain the freedom that we have enjoyed under our Constitution for over 175 years. All the trouble arises from a curious provision in our Constitution, which, up to now, has never been regarded as particularly dangerous. That provision is part of Article 6 of the Constitution which provides, in substance, that all treaties shall be the supreme law of the land, anything in the Constitution or laws of any state to the contrary notwithstanding. This part of the Constitution makes our Supreme Court powerless to do anything about a treaty which contradicts our Constitution or any of our laws. If the United States were to enter into a treaty with a foreign country, granting that country the right to come into your home and take your property, there is no way any court or law could help you. This possibility has existed since the beginning of our country, and perhaps you wonder why nothing has been done for 175 years.

Until about thirty years ago, our Supreme Court, by its decisions, said, in effect, that the United States could not make a treaty that is contrary to our Constitution. In 1920, the Supreme Court changed its mind by an opinion handed down in the case of *Missouri* v. *Holland*. For the first time in the history of this country the Supreme Court permitted the Federal Government to accomplish, under the auspices of a treaty with Canada, what the Constitution did not permit it to do in the absence of a treaty.

Another reason why this part of the Constitution has not been of particular concern until recently, is that for a long time treaties did not affect our normal, everyday lives. Prior to the organization of the United Nations, even lawyers took comparatively little interest in treaties between the United States and foreign countries. The question of trade agreements and boundaries could safely be left to the State Department, the President, and the Senate. When the United Nations was organized in 1945, a new doctrine was announced which stated that treaties should be used to make domestic law as well as international law. This deals with the right of citizens in their relationship to their own government.

Let us look at just one of the treaties being drafted by the United Nations and see how it could affect our lives if ratified by the Senate. There is now in preparation a draft statute for an international criminal court with authority to try American citizens for international crimes. This statute could easily permit American citizens to be tried before that court for criticizing foreign governments or their officials. Article 37 of this statute provides that the trial shall be without a jury. Of the nine judges on this court, at least one of them would be a Communist. Frankly, under these conditions, I would hate to have my liberty at stake before such a court.

Suppose now we analyze the three main sections of the Bricker amendment and see just how they operate to protect American rights and the American form of government against the dangers of treaty law. The first section firmly establishes that the Constitution is the supreme law of our land, and that the rights guaranteed by the Constitution cannot be bargained away by a treaty. A safeguard has always existed in that treaties are not effective until ratified by the Senate. However, in the past, Congress has passed laws which were later held unconstitutional by the Supreme Court. The Supreme Court does not now have the power to declare a treaty unconstitutional, and this necessary power would be granted to that Court under the Bricker amendment.

Section 2 prevents a treaty from becoming effective as internal law in the United States unless it is supplemented by an appropriate law which would be valid in the absence of such a treaty. Under this section of the amendment, a portion of a treaty dealing with international matters will take effect immediately, but any portion that deals with internal law will require additional legislation before it will have any legal effect.

Section 3 grants Congress the power to regulate executive agreements. This section does not tie the hands of the President beyond assuring that he does not, through executive agreements, alter our internal domestic law in a manner the Constitution does not permit of the Congress through legislation. A great deal of criticism has been directed toward section 3 of the Bricker amendment on the ground that the President will be greatly handicapped in making executive agreements. There is nothing in this section which compels Congress to regulate and pass on all executive agreements affecting foreign affairs. Under the amendment, the President can go ahead making executive agreements as freely as heretofore, but the Bricker amendment will authorize Congress to act, when in its judgment it is necessary to protect American interests against a President entering into such far-reaching and disastrous executive agreements as those of Teheran, Yalta, and Potsdam. No longer will any President be able to call a treaty an executive agreement, and thus bypass the Senate and the Congress in committing the United States to international obligations of far-reaching effect.

Some of the people who oppose the Bricker amendment mention the role of the United States in world affairs, and claim that the amendment will hamper our foreign relations. Actually, the amendment safeguards, rather than hampers our conduct with foreign countries. I cannot agree with those who advocate that the world should be one big, happy family. No other country has been so generous as the United States in lending a helping hand to countries in need. Our boys have died on foreign soil in protecting a free way of life.

From time to time we hear proposals stemming from the United Nations that the Americans should embrace some form of world citizenship. I can think of nothing more disastrous than for us to lose our identity as American citizens. There is no way that we can save the world and achieve world peace by giving up American rights and American independence. Our forefathers fought a revolution to become an independent nation. They fought for the right to be governed by laws made by their own elected representatives. If we stand idly by, the United Nations organizations will make our laws through treaties, where the representatives of other nations have a majority voice in what these treaties shall cover, both as to language and as to content. We must not permit our basic right under the Constitution and the Bill of Rights to be rewritten, compromised, and bargained away by United Nations treaties. Whatever we do in world affairs, our first consideration should be the preservation of this country's integrity as a free, solvent, and independent nation. The Bricker amendment, I believe, is a must to help preserve America.

AGAINST THE BRICKER AMENDMENT [10]

Thomas C. Hennings, Jr. [11]

Senator Thomas C. Hennings (Democrat, Missouri) spoke to the Senate against the Bricker amendment just before the vote was taken on February 26, 1954. His was one of the spirited closing arguments given in reply to the debates by such energetic proponents of the measure as Senator Price Daniel (Democrat, Texas). The Missouri Senator, although a newcomer in the Senate, quickly took his place as a sound reasoner, ready debater, and well-grounded student of legal history and processes. As his debate on this subject would indicate, he is an internationalist. (Only the closing part of his argument is here reprinted.)

The second reason for the proposal of the Senator from Georgia, as I understand is his fear that if we do not adopt his amendment or a similar one—which he considers to be, and which actually is, more moderate and reasonable than that proposed by the Senator from Ohio—we shall, in time, be forced to accept some such proposal as the Bricker amendment which would strike at the very heart of our Constitution.

If this be the case, Mr. President, I say let us go to the country. Let the issue be fully debated and understood by the citizens of our country. If, then, the people decide, through political elections, to change the Constitution and to put the President in a straitjacket, then the will of the people will be done and the Constitution, of course, will be changed. I have no fear that this will ever come to pass.

As I have said before, the powers of the Presidency derive from the people, and when the people of this country elected Dwight D. Eisenhower as President of the United States in November 1952, I believe they clearly intended that he should succeed to all the historic and traditional and constitutional powers of all the Presidents who preceded him. I would remind

[10] *Congressional Record.* 100:2233. February 26, 1954 (daily edition). Only the closing section of the argument is here included.

[11] For biographical note, see Appendix.

my Republican friends, in all good feeling and kindness, that President Eisenhower has emphatically stated his opposition to any amendment which would cut down the presidential powers. He has strongly urged us not to paralyze his power to act swiftly and effectively in the national interest. If any of my Republican colleagues persist in voting for this amendment or for any other unacceptable compromise, they will not only repudiate the position of the President of the United States but, I believe, will be casting a clear vote of lack of confidence in the head of their own party. I believe that the American people had no intention of electing a President and thereafter striking down his power or diluting it.

Confident as I am that the American people would soundly reject any such proposal, I am at a loss to understand how we in the Senate of the United States, fully aware of our responsibilities to our nation, can seriously entertain a proposition that might, at times, under certain conditions, paralyze our own foreign policy. What would we achieve if we plow stubbornly ahead and actually tie the hands of the President? Would we have protected our country or our liberties or our people against any danger, real or imagined? In the face of real danger, with the threat of Russian imperialism hanging like a dark cloud over free men everywhere on the globe, have we as Americans no better alternative than to immobilize the Commander in Chief, so that he is powerless to act quickly and effectively in a national emergency? Mr. President, such a solution flies in the face of the law, the facts, and the realities of the world in which we live. We should reject it utterly and completely, once and for all.

As for the dangers which exist mainly in our imagination— and we have heard much talk about threats and possibilitiies—I think it is time that we recognized them for the unsubstantial and chimerical things that they are—albeit they may cloud our vision and, for a time, obscure our judgment. The Senate of the United States stands on trial today before the court of world opinion. If we abandon our historic position, we stand convicted as men of little faith. If we sacrifice statesmanship for expediency, we shall have gained no profit by our barter, and we will have lost immeasurably in stature and prestige throughout the world.

We cannot be driven by a spirit of expediency or the counsel of fear, Mr. President, to accept any proposal. We must not debase the Constitution of the United States by embedding in it some vague words which have no precise meaning to us even now.

In the opinion of many Senators and of many qualified constitutional lawyers and students, this would serve only to open broad areas of doubt and confusion for some unknown and unpredictable future interpretation. When we undertake to improve upon the work of the Founding Fathers, every presumption, in my opinion, should abide with our Constitution as it now stands. We should at this hour remember the Eighteenth Amendment and its unhappy effect upon our country. I hope that we will act with maturity and reason to defend and protect the Constitution of the United States. Let us, by our vigilance, preserve that testament of the faith of a free people. Let us preserve inviolate this charter of our liberties which has been our inspiration for 165 years that it may endure as the foundation stone of our strength in a troubled and perilous world.

INDUSTRY AND LABOR

WHAT KIND OF AMERICA?[1]

BENJAMIN F. FAIRLESS [2]

Benjamin F. Fairless, chairman of the United States Steel Corporation, gave this address before the Economic Club of Detroit, September 21, 1953.

The speech, like Fairless' preceding ones, was well-organized, and centered on a well developed argument and plea—in this case for greater productiveness as the further vindication of private enterprise. Fairless called on producers to reject the unhealthy mood abroad among many businessmen and economists who talked of a possible deep recession. The speaker interpolated his arguments and ample evidence with recurrent admonitions for demonstration of resourceful industry and bold initiative.

Fairless, here as on other occasions, was forthright and vigorous in manner and ideas, and yet anecdotal, and always alert to his audience. Note his highly personal tone (well over sixty *I*'s, and much use of *me, us,* and *you*).

His points were flavored with sharp colloquialisms (*come hell or high water, pulling in their necks, earthbound type of fellow, crawled down into the storm cellar, monetary dope addicts, jerry-built tax structure*). The speaker gave to the familiar ideas supporting private enterprise a fresh twist.

Fairless, in language, ideas, and delivery, ranks with the best of recent business and professional speakers. Others in this area who have been leaders not only in industry but in speaking have included Henry Ford II, Lewis Brown, W. S. Gifford, C. M. Chester, C. F. Kettering, H. W. Prentis, Merle Thorpe, Eric Johnson, Clarence Randall, Owen D. Young, and Robert Young.[3]

That was a wonderful build-up that Harlow Curtice has just given me, and I would be the last man in the world to dispute a single word of it. But just for the sake of his future reputation, I hope that you gentlemen will remember that toastmasters

[1] Text supplied through the courtesy of Benjamin F. Fairless with permission for this reprint.

[2] For biographical note, see Appendix.

[3] For further comment on Fairless, see his "Detour Ahead," *Representative American Speeches: 1949-50*, p 164 ff.

are not expected to stick too closely to the awful truth. They are merely supposed to make their victim feel as happy as possible before he is fed to the lions. And in my case, that has never been done more successfully!

There was one part of his remarks, however, that I liked even more than the others; and that was when he referred to a statement of mine as "Detroit talk." Now, in my book, that is a very great compliment indeed, for it has always seemed to me that whenever Detroit talks, it speaks the economic language of a growing, dynamic America—the kind of America that has confidence in itself and a boundless faith in its future. That is the kind of America I believe in; and it is the kind of talk that I believe in, too.

You see, the automobile industry and I were born at the same time, so I've watched it grow from a pup; and while I've never been a direct part of it, it has taught me a great deal about the true meaning of the word *enterprise*. In fact, you people in Detroit remind me a lot of the old Swedish prospector who went out to California and struck it very, very rich. Every time he disappeared into the hills he came up with a new vein of ore that was even bigger and better than the last one; and his envious companions were trying desperately to learn his secret. Finally, one day, he broke down and told them how he did it:

"Boys," he said, "I yoost keep digging holes."

And that's how it is with you fellows. Come hell or high water, you yoost keep making cars!

Forty years ago, when the old Central Steel Company was being built, and when I got my job there, things generally were pretty tough. Business was suffering from one of those "recessions" that we hear so much talk about these days; and a lot of people were pulling in their necks, cutting down on inventories, laying off men, and waiting around for times to get better.

But in Detroit, of course, you didn't seem to notice the recession. You were far too busy trying to design and build a better automobile. To do that, however, you needed alloy steels, and because of the market you created for them, a little group of men, who spoke your language and believed in it, were able to organize and build the Central Steel Company at a time when other mills, with better equipment, bigger machines, and established markets, were fighting to keep their heads above water.

So if it hadn't been for "Detroit talk," that Central Steel plant near Massillon would never have been built at all; and I would not be a steel man today.

Nor would America be what it is today either; for "Detroit talk" has not only given us the automobile industry—it has fathered the oil industry and the rubber industry; it has provided our largest single market for steel, and it has built the great network of roads and highways that we have today. In short, it has created millions of jobs in almost every conceivable branch of our economic life, and has added billions of dollars to our national income.

Truly it is the language of progress and prosperity; but unhappily it has not yet become the universal language of American business. On many sides of us these days, we still hear a tongue that is wholly foreign to your own—a voice that speaks the language of pessimism, of timidity, of inaction, of alarm and of defeat. And on several occasions that I can remember, these Prophets of Pessimism have beamed their solemn warnings directly at Detroit, just as some of them are doing today.

They have told you that you were overextended; that your markets were saturated, your dealers overstocked, and that you were riding for a fall. But you wouldn't listen. You wouldn't slow down. You had to go right ahead making more and more cars, while your customers—for some strange reason that the prophets have never explained—went right ahead buying them. And so far, you've always been right. I happen to think that you're still right!

So it's a great pleasure and a welcome relief for me to be able to visit you in this Oasis of Optimism. I can think of no more appropriate time or place to unburden myself of one or two things that I've been wanting to get off my chest for quite a while, and I'm deeply grateful to all of you for giving me this opportunity to do so.

First let me say, however, that I am neither an economist nor a soothsayer, and therefore I do not profess to be able to look into the future and tell you what is going to happen next month or next year. I'm just the plodding, earth-bound type of fellow who believes that our economy will be a whole lot better off in the long run if we spend less time trying to read the future and more energy trying to make the future.

So I shall not add to the general confusion of the day by venturing my predictions of my own, however cheering they might be; but I would like to express a few very definite views about the present situation.

And frankly, I have been considerably concerned and completely perplexed by these pessimistic predictions of a coming recession. Everywhere we turn these days, we hear people asking whether there is going to be one, when it will come and how bad it will be. Some of our most learned and respected economists have come up with a wide variety of answers that run the entire gamut from *yes* to *no;* and the stock market seems to have given up the ghost completely and crawled down into the storm cellar for the duration.

Now I happen to believe very deeply that the kind of America we shall live in tomorrow depends primarily on the kind of a job that we do today. I think that the future of American business can be anything we want to make it; but certainly we shall never achieve the kind of future that you and I want in this country by following a policy of timidity, indecision and inaction. It will take the very best we've got in the way of initiative, enterprise, energy, and—above all—sound judgment.

It seems to me, therefore, that this is a mighty good time to stop and take stock of our present situation. The summer is over. Most of us are planning our product lines and production schedules for the coming winter; but before we make up our minds where we're going, the important thing is to find out where we stand.

So let's take a good look at these gloomy predictions. Let's ask ourselves if they're justified. Let's examine their full implications. Let's try to see them in their true perspective and view them in the light of reason.

Now the most important factor that confronts us as we review our present situation is undoubtedly the great change that has occurred in the economic and political climate in which business operates. In fact I suppose that the past few months have brought the greatest change that we have ever seen in so short a space of time.

For the first time in twenty years, the Washington trend towards socialism has been reversed. The government has begun to withdraw from competition with private enterprise. Price and wage controls have been lifted and a free market has been restored. Inflation has been sharply checked. The cost of living index shows that we have an honest dollar again—a dollar that will buy almost exactly as much today as it did twelve months ago. And most important of all, of course, is the truce in Korea.

In short, we not only have peace—uneasy as that peace may be—but we also have, perhaps, a greater freedom of enterprise than we have enjoyed at any time in the past two decades. These are the things we have hoped for, fought for, and prayed for, these many weary years; but to our utter amazement we now discover that they are the very same things that our pessimists cite in justification of their gloomy predictions. They tell us that just because we do have peace, and an honest dollar, a recession is inevitable.

So if we analyze these predictions and study their full implications, we find, I think, that what the pessimists are really saying is this: that war and inflation are essential to America's prosperity, and that without these two things we cannot maintain our maximum standard of living.

I know that all of us renounce that philosophy with every ounce of plain, old-fashioned common sense that we possess. I don't believe we can ever increase our national wealth by spending the blood of our youth on some battlefield, or by exhausting our natural resources on the engines of war. War never enriches nations; it impoverishes them.

Neither do I believe that Ameirca can ever increase its economic health by becoming a nation of monetary dope addicts. These repeated injections of printing press money may give us a temporary illusion of prosperity; but in the end they can only undermine our fiscal health and security by eating away the savings of our people and by cheating the millions of patriotic men and women who have bought defense bonds.

No one can convince me, therefore, that sound money is a threat to American prosperity, and no one can make me believe that American business, which did such a magnificent job under the pressures of war, is unable to meet successfully the challenge of peace!

For a number of years, a great many of us have been telling the American people that the only basic essential of a healthy, prosperous, steadily-growing economy is a free system of enterprise—a system of private initiative and incentive, with free competitive markets, an honest dollar, and a chance to direct its industrial might into peaceful channels of production.

Well, to a very large degree, at least, we now have what we asked for. We have the basic essentials; and it's up to us to deliver. Nor do I have the slightest doubt of our ability to do so. To my way of thinking, American business today has the greatest and most challenging opportunity that has come its way in twenty years.

This is our chance, and we can't afford to muff it; for nothing on earth could possibly give more aid and comfort to our Communist enemies abroad, and to our Socialist-minded friends here at home, than a first-class recession in America. Their only hope is that the sudden ending of war and inflation will send our economy into a tailspin. Then they can tell the world that free enterprise was the cause of it all.

But their hope is fading fast. The only real glimmer that remains is the chance that we may yet "predict" ourselves into a recession; and I believe we could do just that.

If I were a Socialist, and if I wanted to discredit the free enterprise sysytem by producing a serious business slump, I think I would start predicting from the housetops that hard times were on their way. And if I could shout long enough and loud enough, and could get other people to take up my mournful cry, I think I could frighten millions of customers right out of the market place.

I think I could scare them into hoarding their money instead of spending it on a new house or a new car or on most of the other things they had planned to buy this year. In the same way, to, I think I might persuade a number of businessmen to become jittery and overcautious—to postpone the introduction of new models and new products, to cut back their expenses, deplete their inventories, curtail their research programs and pare down their payrolls. And if I could get enough customers and enough businessmen to believe me, we would very shortly have a sure-enough recession on our hands; and I would be a great prophet, a friend of the people, and a shoo-in for public office.

But the distressing fact today is that many of the gloomy predictions that we hear from time to time are not coming primarily from our Socialist-minded friends at all, but often from reputable economists and from business and financial experts who honestly want a free enterprise system.

Now it is a little hard for me, of course, to understand how anyone who believes in a free economy in theory, can show so little faith in it in practice; but I want to make it perfectly clear that I do not challenge the sincerity, the integrity or the professional ability of these gentlemen in any way. I do, however, question their perspective, their sense of proportion and their terminology.

And to illustrate what I mean, let me turn for a moment to the only field in which I feel that I am qualified to debate the merit of their conclusions:

One of the barometers upon which these gentlemen rely heavily in preparing their forecasts of the economic weather is the operating rate in the steel industry. That, of course, is an excellent barometer, and it has been falling recently. Except when strikes have interfered, the steel industry has been running for many months at 100 per cent of capacity or better; but in June, the rate dropped below the 100 mark and has never since climbed back to that level. Last month, this barometer stood just under 95, and I judge that it will probably average somewhere in that general neighborhood for the rest of the year.

So our economic weather men are entirely correct when they say that steel production has fallen off; but it seems to me that they have become so obsessed with this downward trend, that they've lost all sense of proportion.

The truth is, of course, that on the basis of present orders, and barring unforeseen work stoppages, the American steel industry will produce, and will sell, more steel this year than ever before, in war or in peace, at any time in its history. In fact, present indications are that it will make about seven million tons more steel than it made in the all-time record year of 1951.

And if that's what our weather men mean by the word "recession," I can only say that the employees and the stockholders of U. S. Steel would like to see that kind of a recession for the rest of their natural lives.

You and I realize, of course, that steel plants were never intended nor designed to operate regularly at 100 per cent of capacity. Historically the steel industry has always had to maintain a substantial reserve of capacity for use in times of great national emergency; and at such times, it is able to run at 100 per cent only by resorting to the uneconomic use of marginal facilities, materials and manpower.

Even during the war-time years of 1941 to 1945—when we were breaking our necks to produce every pound of steel that we could, and when the plants of United States Steel alone were outproducing all the Axis nations put together—the average operating rate for the industry as a whole was just 94 per cent of capacity—or almost exactly what it was last month.

But remember, of course, that our total capacity in those days was much smaller than it is now; and even if our operating rate today were to drop as low as 81 per cent of present capacity, we would still be producing, and selling, more steel than we did all through those frenzied years of World War II.

So it seems to me that these fellows who are so alarmed by the recent trend in steel are a lot like the restaurant owner who was complaining to a customer about how terrible business was. The customer was very much surprised.

"Why look, Joe," he said, "every table in the place is filled and I've seen you turn away at least a dozen people while I've been sitting here."

"I know," said the gloomy proprietor, "but six months ago I was turning away three dozen!"

Well, as a steel man, I've learned to my sorrow, these last few years, that you can't make a profit on the business you turn away; and that's why I think that our present-day pessimists should develop a little perspective as they analyze these trends. I also think they should define their terms, because to the average American, the word *recession* is merely economic double talk meaning *depression*. It is the exact opposite of the word *prosperity*, and it is certainly a far cry from any business situation that now exists or that is likely to exist so far as I can see.

In saying that, I am not trying to minimize the importance or the significance of trends; but as a businessman, there is one statistic in which I put more faith than in any other—and that is the condition of the American consumer's pocketbook.

Today more people have jobs in America than ever before in our history—about 63.5 million of them, in fact. They are also getting the highest wages in history. Personal income of the American people as a whole stands at an all-time peak. They are spending more money than ever before; and in spite of all they are spending, they still managed to save the fabulous sum of $17 billion last year.

The market is there, and the money is there, and all in the world we have to do is go out and get it! I know of course, that our Prophets of Pessimism are terribly worried by the fact that there is no pent-up, postwar backlog of consumer demand as there was at the end of World War II. But do you believe for a minute that all of these millions of people, with all of these billions of dollars in their pockets, have already bought everything they need and want?

Well, neither do I. If the product is right and the price is right, they are ready and able to buy it. We only have to make what they want; and to make them want what we make. So what our pessimists are really talking about is not recession at all. It is nothing more nor less than plain, old-fashioned competition, with plenty of enterprise and salesmanship. And that's right down our alley!

To sum it all up, therefore, let me put it this way:

For nearly fifteen years, this nation has been out on an economic bender of very large proportions, and in the process, it has consumed intoxicating quantities of war, inflation, government handouts, deficit spending, ruinous taxation and predatory politics. And now it has come to the inevitable morning after.

Well, you don't get over a party like that without having some kind of a hangover—or at least, so I've been told. There are just naturally bound to be headaches, dislocations and readjustments; but let's recognize the headaches for what they really are: the pains produced by past excesses and not the symptoms of some impending economic disease. We are not sickening; we are recovering, and we have nothing to fear except, perhaps, the blandishments of our Socialist-minded friends who will be back in full force next year trying to persuade us to take just one more little nip of the hair of the dog that bit us!

But the only real cure for what ails us is plenty of exercise and hard work.

Now all of us realize, of course, that many of the economic difficulties we see around us are properly the concern of government, and that it is not within our power, as individuals, to correct them.

We know that our jerry-built tax structure needs a complete overhaul job, so that the enormous revenues which our government must have, can be raised without destroying the incentive of our people to produce more and to buy more.

We know that farm income is declining; and that no one has yet devised a government price-support program that will promote readjustment instead of perpetuating maladjustment.

And we know that millions of people in foreign lands are eager and anxious to buy American products, but are not permitted by their governments to do so.

A proper solution of these problems in Washington would give a magnificent lift to the whole level of business activity; but much as I want to see these problems solved, I do not share the unreasoning impatience of some of my fellow citizens who have been so critical of congressional delay in acting upon them.

It seems to me that one of our major difficulties stems from the fact that these important issues have, for twenty years, been the subject of ill-considered, stopgap legislation that was jammed through the mill under the pressure of constant crisis and emergency. Now for the first time they are being subjected to thoughtful and exhaustive study by committees of conscientious and capable men; and I, for one, am willing to await the findings and recommendations of these committees, for it had never occurred to me to expect that all of the evils of the past would or could be corrected in the space of a few months.

But important as government action will be in its influence upon our general economy, the task of shaping America's future still rests, I believe, primarily on the American producer. So what are we waiting for?

We know what kind of America we want—an America that is free, peaceful and prosperous—a land of ever-growing opportunity with a constantly-rising standard of living for all of our people in every walk of life.

That is the kind of America which our forefathers built and handed down to us. It is the kind of America we have today. It is the kind of America we hope—with God's help—to keep.

But that kind of America was never built—or kept—by men of little faith. It was built by men of courage and daring who had confidence in themselves and who were willing to risk their fortunes and their lives for what they wanted. In no other spirit could our American system have been conceived, and in no other spirit can it survive.

So I repeat, it's up to us. We can have the kind of America we want if we have the enterprise, the courage and the faith to do so. We cannot afford to be overcautious and afraid; nor can we afford, of course, to throw caution to the winds, for sound business judgment was never more necessary than it is today.

But all in the world we really need is less pessimism, more "Detroit talk" and a full realization of the fact that nobody has yet made a dime by selling America short!

LABOR DAY MESSAGE [4]

George Meany [5]

President George Meany, of the American Federation of Labor, gave this address to the nation, over the Columbia Broadcasting System at 10:45 P.M., E.S.T., on Monday, Setpember 7, 1953. The speaker talked from Washington, D.C.

President Meany wasted no time in unfolding his theme. His method was that of a chain of reasoning: (1) To deal with the Russian hydrogen bomb menace we must have production. (2) Such production depends upon efficient labor. (3) Efficient labor depends upon proper conservation of the labor supply. (4) Conservation of labor depends upon some six elements (not properly handled by the Republican administration): (a) the control of inflation, (b) housing, (c) social security, (d) reduced costs of medical care, (e) proper educational facilities, (f) repeal of the Taft-Hartley law. Whether Meany's indictment of the Eisenhower administration was justified would depend upon what the Eighty-third Congress, convening in its second session, in January 1954, would do. With the 1954 election looming, that body proposed to make much effort to deal with those six "glaring weaknesses in our national life."

Meany, in his economic philosophy and union methods, is the direct heir of Samuel Gompers. Meany was hardly out of his teens when his forceful speaking drew attention of the unionists to him. He successively held more important elective offices in his craft union federation, culminating in his election in November 1952, to the presidency, successor to the deceased William Green. Meany's platform force and aggressive personality largely account for his rise. Without great heat in delivery, and without the vocabulary richness of John L. Lewis, Meany has talked in forthright phrases and with vocal naturalness that have commanded the respect and attention not only of the "nine millions" of the AFL, but of many other American listeners.

Labor Day is the one national holiday which does not commemorate famous heroes or historic events. It is dedicated to the millions of men and women who work for wages, the people who have built America's towns and cities, the skilled and

---

[4] Text and permission for this reprint furnished through the courtesy of George Meany and the national office of the American Federation of Labor.

[5] For biographical note, see Appendix.

unskilled laborers who are responsible, in large measure, for the miracle of American industrial progress.

As the representative of nine million of these working men and women, it is my purpose to report to you on the issues which are of supreme importance on this Labor Day.

First comes the issue of war or peace. It was not resolved by the truce negotiated in Korea. That event has failed to ease the growing international tension caused by Soviet Russia's relentless determination to dominate and control the entire world.

Since the death of Stalin, sweet words have been broadcast by his successors in the Kremlin, but they mean absolutely nothing in the way of concrete assurance of peace. The grim facts are clear. The Russian dictators may change their tactics, but they have not changed their objective. They still refuse to enter into any enforceable agreement for disarmament. They still refuse to give up the use of war of aggression. They even refuse to work out reasonable peace treaties necessary to end chaotic conditions left over from the last World War.

To these ominous factors, something new had been added. The Communists have proved they now possess the secret of the hydrogen bomb—the world's most dreaded weapon.

What does atomic war mean? It means that a million people —men, women and children—can be wiped out of existence in a few seconds by a single bomb blast. It means that whole cities, with most of their population, can be reduced to ashes overnight.

To us that kind of warfare is unthinkable. Labor builds. It does not destroy. The thought of having our entire civilization go up in smoke appears to us nothing short of madness.

How can we prevent such a war? Our national leaders have explored every conceivable way to induce the Communists to listen to reason and used every possible approach to bring about peace by negotiation without concrete results. It would be folly to suppose that appeasement would provide a solution. No dictator in history has ever been converted to human decency by appeasement. Partial surrender to the insatiable demands of the Communists can only lead eventually to total surrender.

The only thing they fear or respect is superior power. The only factor that will deter them from plunging the world into another war is the knowledge that they will have to contend against superior power.

How does America stand? Do we possess greater power than the Soviet empire? If not, how can we achieve it?

It is not my purpose to compare the military might of the free world with that of the Communists. That is not my field. In modern warfare, the prime factor actually is the ability to produce. And in that respect, America enjoys at this time definite superiority.

When reduced to essentials, production depends upon men and machines and raw material. We have the skilled manpower. We have the machines. And we possess, or have thus far been able to import from the free world, all the materials we need.

Some of our military strategists believe that the production problem of greatest concern is access to raw materials. I disagree. All the materials in the world and all the machines in the world put together would produce nothing without a capable, a loyal and a willing work force.

Thus the human element is obviously the main element in the national defense picture. And that is why, by all means, we should concentrate on strengthening the status and the security of the working men and women who serve in the front lines of our defense production program.

On this Labor Day, the American worker stands head and shoulders above the workers of any other land. His wages and working conditions are better. He and his family have better homes to live in, better food to eat and better clothing. These advances did not come to the workers of our country automatically. They were won by organizing into trade unions and by struggle against stubborn opposition.

Because they are better off, the workers of America produce more than workers in other countries, who do not possess the skill, the training nor the incentive to get ahead. By the same token, the high standards enjoyed by American workers create the mass purchasing power which has made it possible for industry to grow and expand to a productive capacity unmatched anywhere on earth.

This is the bright side of the picture. But there is another side. There are glaring weaknesses in our national life which require immediate action, vulnerable spots which demand correction if we hope to muster our total strength for the long-drawn-out struggle ahead.

Let's get down to cases. First is the basic problem of inflation. Higher wages don't buy any more groceries when the cost of living keeps climbing to record heights. When the Eighty-third Congress abolished economic controls and killed rent controls, we were told that prices could more effectively be stabilized by indirect methods. Well, those methods haven't worked. The working people of this country and the farmers as well, are being victimized by unjustifiable profiteering. It must be stopped. It is up to Congress to halt inflation if the nation is to be kept strong.

The second problem is housing. At least eight million of our people are still living in the worst kind of slums—slums that breed disease, juvenile delinquency and crime. Yet the Eighty-third Congress cut off the low-cost, public housing program which is the only effective method of replacing slums with decent housing for those in the lowest income brackets.

Even families with moderate incomes cannot buy the homes they need at prices they can afford. The government increased interest rates to the bankers on home loans, but it took no action to meet the housing shortage. At the rate our population is growing, the country will need 12 million new housing units in the next six years. To prevent needless suffering and to keep the American people strong, Congress should act promptly to encourage the building industry to meet this acute deficiency.

Another field, in which we have gone backward instead of forward, is social security. This is the self-insurance program through which our country has sought to protect the American people from fear of unemployment and fear of destitute old age. It has served also as a powerful bulwark to economic stability and the security of the free enterprise system itself.

But what has happened to social security? Millions of Americans are still left unprotected. Inflation, with its fifty-cent dollar, has cut benefits below the minimum subsistence level. Almost 10 per cent of our people have now reached the legal retirement age of sixty-five. Millions more are approaching old age in fear of poverty.

To afford them the security which they were promised and for which they paid insurance, through payroll taxes, Congress is duty-bound to improve the social security program. Yet it has done nothing but to postpone action.

The record of the Eighty-third Congress on health problems is even worse. It refused to give any consideration whatsoever to the growing need for a national program to insure the American people against the high cost of medical care. It took no action on bipartisan appeals for aid to medical schools so that the alarming shortage of doctors, nurses and hospital facilities could be overcome.

Obviously, Congress has failed to meet human needs in the vital field of social security and health. It has failed to strengthen the nation.

When it comes to the need for education, there can be no controversy. The facts speak for themselves. The Federal Commissioner of Education only a few days ago reported shocking conditions in American schools due to reopen this month, after summer vacations. There is a tremendous shortage of school space for our children. One out of every five will be exposed to the danger of fire-traps. There are not enough teachers to go around. The shortage of 72,000 teachers is due to the fact that teachers' salaries have been allowed to sink shamefully low.

This is the official record. Congress knows all the facts. The members of Congress understand, as well as you or I, the prime importance to our national vitality and safety of good education for the nation's children. Yet what has it done about this basic problem of Federal aid to education? Absolutely nothing. Surely, in the field of education, our nation must be greatly strengthened.

Finally, we are still faced with the serious problems arising from the manifest unfairness of the Taft-Hartley Act to the nation's workers. Because it is weighted against labor, this law can—at any time—throw production schedules out of balance. This fact is clear to the responsible leaders of our nation. In his first message to Congress, President Eisenhower said that the law must be changed to eliminate union-busting provisions and to provide a fair and just code for the guidance of labor-management relations. Yet, after months of public hearings, Congress did nothing. Unless Congress fulfills its responsibility to act constructively on this issue at its next session, our nation will not be able to achieve its maximum production strength for survival against the threat of Communist dictatorship.

Let me make one thing clear. Congress will not act on any or all of these problems until and unless the people of this country demand action. Your Congress represents you. Under our democracy, you can make your government carry out your wishes or you can vote it out of office. The power to give America the power it needs is in your hands.

This is not the situation behind the Iron Curtain. Under the Soviet dictatorship, the people of Russia and its satellites have no will of their own. They must obey orders or die.

As we see it, the fatal weakness in Soviet Russia's armor is the enforced slavery of its people. When the test comes, slaves will never stand up under pressure like free men. This is not wishful thinking. It was proven in the last World War. It was proven all over again on June 17.

On that date, the whole world caught its first glimpse of the true conditions behind the Iron Curtain. Through the open window of East Berlin, we saw slave workers rise up against their oppressors and dare to fight guns and tanks with their bare fists. Since then, resentment of the workers against intolerable conditions has spread like wildfire throughout the satellite states. As soon as one uprising is suppressed, another springs up. The Communists cannot depend upon the loyalty and support of the people they have enslaved. They are hated.

We, in the American Federation of Labor, want no part of communism. Experience has taught us that free labor can exist and make progress only in a free land. There is no stronger enemy of communism in the world than the nine million men and women who make up the A.F.L.

Our hopes and objectives on this Labor Day can be summed up briefly. We want to make America strong so that it can continue to be free. We want to build up the whole fabric of our national life, so that the freedoms which all of us cherish can survive and endure.

WHO ARE THE AMERICANS OF TODAY? [6]

John L Lewis [7]

John L. Lewis, president of the United Mine Workers of America, gave this address before the Chicago Executives' Club, Chicago, Illinois, on June 5, 1953. His audience was composed largely of business leaders, including some who had argued vigorously at the conference table with the United Mine Workers' spokesman.

The address was typical of Lewis' skill in marshaling arguments, but dressing them with facts, and couching the ideas in language sometimes formal and rhetorical (*e.g.,* "I have a matutinal indisposition that emanates from the nauseous effluvia of the slave statute—the Taft-Hartley Act").

The introduction was conciliatory, with its tribute to the audience, its recital of the mine workers' recent history, and its statement of issues. The argument proper was compact, blunt, and unfolded deductively, with little design to continue the conciliation of the preliminary passages.

In essence the logical steps (each open to much criticism) were: (1) The Taft-Hartley Act is crippling labor. (2) Labor's full protection is essential to the efficient functioning of the American economic system. (3) That system is in grave danger—through the possible decline of defense spending; through the rising threats of competition from Soviet communism (*e.g.,* Soviet penetration of Latin America); through our failure to build up foreign trade by proper distribution of our goods and services (*e.g.,* coal) rather than by our handing out of dollars. (4) To ensure full economic health within our country and in our foreign economic dealings, we must not "annihilate each other." Rather we must work together (*i.e.,* repeal the Taft-Hartley Act). This fourth proposition was implied but not developed. The conclusion was swift— as if the speaker's time ran out before he had enforced the full consequence of his argument.

Lewis, in his seventy-third year, continued his vigorous platform leadership and committee negotiations related to his union. He has long been recognized as a first-rate orator. As speaker he was more effective than the late Samuel Gompers, William Green, Matthew Woll, or perhaps Philip Murray. Lewis belongs to the older school of political oratory, that of Bryan more than of Franklin Roosevelt and the later radio and television personalities. Lewis in delivery has been bold, even brilliant,

---

[6] Permission for this reprint was granted through the courtesy of John L. Lewis. Text is from the version published and distributed by Labor's Non-Partisan League.

[7] For biographical note, see Appendix.

at home with a wide vocabulary, strong in invective, and powerful in less emotional expression. His voice, in his more dramatic moments, has been strong, intense, and rich in overtones.[8]

Mr. President, Officers and Members of the Executives' Club, Distinguished Guests:

I suppose I have been a long time coming here. But it is generally known that I was detained either by an industrialist or a federal judge. And as I look back on those numerous detentions through the years I am not right now clear as to how they all came out. At least, however, I am happy that time and circumstance have permitted me to be your guest at this magnificent meeting of your great club. The Executives' Club of Chicago is one of the nation's great forums and has been made so by its interest in public and national affairs, by the vigor and ability of its members, their mobility of thought, and their desires constantly to break new ground in the affairs of the nation and of the world. So I come here today by invitation and with gratification that circumstances have permitted me to come on this occasion. I am delighted with your hospitality. I shall speak to you merely as a fellow American.

I am particularly happy to see present here today so many of the towering figures of one of our great basic industries—the coal industry—whom I have valued as friends and adversaries, wise counselors and earnest men, who have been constantly working through the years to make a contribution not only to their own personal well-being, but to the public weal. As I look upon them here today and greet them, I am happy to think that they have honored me with their attendance at this luncheon to join with us in any discussion that may ensue affecting those problems that are so important to every American.

The coal industry, by the way, if I may say a word in passing, is a great basic industry representing a vast investment operating and contributing to our welfare in many states. It performs one of the greatest public services of any industry or any segment of our population in times of national emergency. In two World

[8] For further comment on Lewis as speaker, see *Representative American Speeches: 1940-41*, p 113-24; *1945-46*, p 180-95.

Wars it has expanded its production to meet all of the extra domestic requirements, incident to war and preparations for war. And in addition it has been able to furnish enough coal to the Allies of our nation to keep their economies functioning and to permit them to participate to the maximum degree in their own war effort.

In World War I the bituminous coal industry had more than 700,000 men engaged in that enterprise. It expanded its production as required. It received no government aid or subsidy. Private enterprise performed the job necessary to be performed in a time of national peril. In World War II with 300,000 less men than during the period of World War I it produced some 120 million tons more, during the peak period, than it did during the similar period of World War I, showing progress, showing increase of productivity, showing high efficiency. This is a tribute to the management of the industry, to the engineering genius of the industry and to the manpower of the industry and the collective bargaining structure that made that record possible. All of this was done without the cost of a dollar to the American taxpayer at a time when nearly every industry could claim an element of defense was carried, to a greater or lesser degree, at the expense of the public treasury—either directly or indirectly.

It is a tribute to that spirit of America which first created this republic of ours, which cared for it during the intervening decades of time and which is now charged with the responsibility of its protection in the future. This is a load and a responsibility, by the way, that increases day by day in this time of world stress, world caviling and world confusion. As compared with the other countries of the world, the American coal mining industry is something of which to be proud. In relation to any coal producing country in Europe or elsewhere, I might put its accomplishments on a thumb-nail basis and say that it produces coal at seven times the daily productive capacity for each man employed as compared with the old world, with a wage structure that is five times as great on a daily or weekly basis, at a cost which is only one third of the cost per ton at pithead of these nations. There's the record of the American coal industry.

The manpower engaged in our bituminous industry is the equivalent of the manpower engaged in the coal industry of Japan. And while our manpower produced more than 600 million tons in one year, the best that Japan has been able to do, with a similar work force, is to produce 36 or 37 million tons in one year. There's the record of progress; there's the record of cooperation; there's the record of collective bargaining. The advances in the wage structure and in the living standards, the holding down of the unit cost per ton, the return to the investor in the industry—all these have been accomplished out of the new values inherent in increased productivity per man employed.

I felt that on this occasion and in the presence of these distinguished leaders of the coal industry it was incumbent upon me merely to cite those facts in passing. And if it be true that during these years the welkin has rung upon occasion with the noises that emanated from our joint conferences in the industry when we enthusiastically disagreed upon some subject, it has only been the bargaining in the market place under a system of free enterprise.

And since time first was, the right to bargain in the market place and the right to sell or not to sell or the right to buy or withhold from buying has been inherently one of the privileges of free men. It is one of the basic factors for a continuation of our free enterprise system in our own country. Limit the right of the buyer to buy or not to buy, limit the right of the seller to sell or not to sell and you strike a blow at the free enterprise system, call it what you will—capitalism, investment for profit, whatever you want to name it. There is the difference between the more absolute forms of government and that scheme of government set up in our own country by the fathers of the nation who handed it to us as their stewards to see if we could keep what they gave us.

It is inherently true in all the material affairs of life that an individual faces two great tasks: First, to acquire something or accomplish something; and second to try to keep it. And that's the obligation upon America today. Can we keep this nation of ours? Can we retain free enterprise? Can we offset and resist the rising, threatening tide of the world communism? Can we

resist the tendency in a republic such as our own, to adopt the
devices of the more absolute forms of government, seeking to
justify ourselves in so doing that we are saving the basic concepts
of the republic? That's the job that we face today.

Like you, and all other Americans, I am concerned with the
problems of today and the problems that I foresee for tomorrow.
Free enterprise, our form of government, the American standard
of living, the reward for initiative, ability to unlock the secrets
of the future through our engineering talents, and with the help
of our scientists and students, are at stake in the free world. In
Europe, in Asia, in Africa, in the Antipodes, everywhere on the
globe there is unrest with an expanding population crying for
more food, for greater markets and a greater place in the sun.

And in some respects our own country, standing here upon
the pinnacle of culture and living standards and accomplishments
in the material and in the scientific world, reminds me of Charles
Russell's painting "The Last of Five Thousand." I think we do
not need to be the last of five thousand, providing Americans
work together in common for the preservation of this republic
which we have wrought and these objectives which we have obtained and do not divide our strength and intensify and com-
pound confusion in our body social, economic and politic by
constant contention among ourselves and the following altruistic
will-o'-the-wisps that lead us nowhere except into that wilderness
of unsolved and more or less unsolvable questions that afflict other
countries in the world.

Who are the Americans of today? The Americans of today
are the peoples of every segment of our population. They don't
all dwell in palaces nor in hovels. They are engaged in every
enterprise. They are associated together in our voluntary associations for the promotion of their own particular enterprise in
association with their fellows and under a presumed equality
before the law. They are the ones who must protect our nation
in the future. They are the people whose sons must fight the
wars and whose daughters must nurse the maimed and the injured
and physical wrecks that come from the battlefields. And no
segment of our society, no group of our citizens has any claim
for special consideration in that degree; because that's the duty

that falls upon all of us, whether we are members of the Executives' Club, the National Association of Manufacturers, the American Federation of Labor or one of the Railroad Brotherhoods, or whether we belong to the Onion Growers Association of Illinois, or the Lettuce Growers Association of the Imperial Valley, or the Cotton Growers of the South or the Hog Growers of Illinois.

We have a common destiny, a common welfare, a common obligation. And it is incumbent upon all of us to recognize the privileges and the rights of others similarly engaged, similarly dedicated and similarly resolved to protect this political, social and economic edifice for the coming generations.

That's one reason why every day I have a matutinal indisposition that emanates from the nauseous effluvia of that oppressive slave statute—the Taft-Hartley Act. It's oppressive legislation against a segment of our population, equally important with any other segment. It's the first step toward oppressive government. And some of you who are students will recall that Confucius said that oppressive government was more to be feared than tigers. I fear oppressive government. So did the framers of our Constitution fear oppressive government. So did the stewards who maintained that Constitution through these decades of time also fear oppressive government.

The Taft-Hartley Act makes me a second class citizen because I represent a labor organization. You know in all confidence I resist the right of Taft to make me a second-class citizen. I don't think he has the right, nor has anyone associated with him. As an American I don't expect to yield him that right. And I represent a lot of people who have authorized me to continue in that attitude. And to put it very conservatively that's what I expect to do. The Taft-Hartley Act was designed first to make more difficult the taking of new blood into labor unions. Secondly, it contains devices to harass those labor unions through the secondary boycott sections and the damage suit sections. And thirdly, it was designed as an instrument to eliminate labor unions in the event that we have an opportune time for their elimination such as another depression. It is punitive. It is a modern bill of attainder written in modern language to fit modern conditions.

I think it is a detriment and a threat to everything we stand for in America.

With our expanding economy and with our highly integrated and complex economy, with 70 per cent of our expanding population living in urban centers, it is not possible for the National Association of Manufacturers or the United States Chamber of Commerce or the Committee for Constitutional Government to exercise all of the powers of free citizenship in America. And it is not possible to dream of the elimination of labor unions in America in our form of economy and to think at the same time that the Republic will endure.

Those who have read the history of the ancient guilds in the Low Countries and in England know that those guilds, which reached a position of great influence and public service in the stabilization of the economy of those countries, were gradually interdicted out of existence by the Taft-Hartleyites of that day and age. And those blind adherents of that form of oppressive legislation, who would willingly use and exercise such a dreadful weapon upon our modern labor unions today, little understand the confusion and chaos that would ensue in economic America were the labor unions to be eliminated as a factor in our economic and social enterprise.

We have a free economy. And our free economy can only function so long as our ever-increasing units of production find a market for their goods. With productivity per-man-employed increasing every day through the genius of our scientists and engineers and chemists and management, with the total labor force being augmented every year, increasing and increasing and increasing the total volume of production that awaits shipment to the markets, there is no market for those goods except a constantly increasing internal market within the confines of the United States and its insular possessions. The world has never been able to take from our shores more than 6 or 8 per cent of our manufactured and fabricated commodities. It's never been able to take more than 10 per cent of our agricultural products. This conversely means that we have to establish buying power in our own country sufficient to move that volume of goods so that factories may work and dividends be paid and buying power be kept up in the market place so that the ever increasing quantity of goods will find a natural usage.

How does this come about? It comes about through the natural and inherent checks and balances in our economic system. They are just as essential to stability in our land as are the checks and balances inherent in our political system, represented by the legislative, judicial and executive branches of government.

The checks and balances in our economy are the labor unions, with collective bargaining power, the voluntary associations— such as the cooperative agency, the onion grower, the hog grower, and whatever form of voluntary association people utilize to bargain in the modern way to achieve buying power and maintain a standard of living, to go on with the dreams that Americans dream. You know what happened in 1929. From 1923 on, we had an era of intense productivity, manufacturing productivity. The volume of our output constantly increased. The number gainfully employed increased, but we had a weak and futile labor movement practically limited to the skilled organizations, with the exception, perhaps, of part of the mining industry.

And labor lacked collective bargaining power in those years from 1922 to 1929, where production and output was constantly increasing the buying power of that part of the population gainfully employed, and subsidiary thereto, those professionally and clerically employed. It was not keeping pace with the production, and the inevitable happend. Orders to ship goods slowed up, and men were laid off. Community buying power dropped and we had a depression. The great productive machine started to move in reverse, and as unemployment became intensified and buying power continuously dropped off, a crisis occurred in our country that took us long, long years to resolve and from which to escape. It was only by artificial stimulation, superinduced by certain government action in the thirties that we finally were able to start the great production machine in the other direction.

That is what caused the depression of 1929. Listen to the economists all you will, read the treatise that you care to read; and the inescapable conclusion of those who lived through that period and who understand something about the integration of our American economy—it will add up simply that the buying power of the American people was insufficient to buy that 90 per cent of our production which we couldn't export, and that the inevitable happened.

What of tomorrow? What of tomorrow? Our nation now has to learn whether or not it can operate under a peacetime economy. We have had more or less of an easy way in recent years as far as any material questions are concerned, because we have had the artificial stimulation of our economy and its business enterprises through the vast sums being spent by the government for indulging in war or preparation for war, and for the rehabilitation of stricken peoples. The only thing that stopped America from going into a tailspin, in reverse, has been the fact that we have given away, under our foreign policy, billions and billions of dollars worth of American output that otherwise would have piled up in our factory warehouses.

But what happens when peace comes, if peace comes? What happens when rehabilitated peoples no longer need our free goods but are engaged in production and manufacture of their own account, and are seeking markets the world over with their particular outputs.

Those of you who have outlets in South America now know that the South American trade is shrinking as far as America is concerned. You know the competition is getting keener in world markets, and that the export of goods from American enterprises abroad—with the exception of a few mass-production industries, all specialized heavy equipment industries—is constantly shrinking, bringing home again, how are you going to keep up buying power in America under peacetime conditions when, at the same time, you pass oppressive labor statutes like the Taft-Hartley Act, designed to weaken, disintegrate and, mayhap, in the end, destroy these great economic devices?

You know, we have been spending money to hire people the world over to oppose communism, and the answer is, of course, that you can't hire a man to oppose an idea in which he may believe, and expect him to work at the job, any longer than you pay him. Meaning—what happens when you quit paying him?

World communism is on the march. It is prevalent in South America, which is in our own hemisphere, and where the policies we have followed have been stupid as far as the material welfare of America is concerned. South America isn't buying goods in American markets, with American dollars, if she can buy those goods more cheaply in the Mediterranean or the Baltic or in Asia.

Last year—1952—Brazil, a great, free South American nation, failed by $236 million to buy as much goods of the United States as we bought from Brazil and for which we paid her dollars. She took that $236 million and she shopped in the cheapened markets in the world—Japan, India, Italy, France, the Low Countries, Holland, Germany, the Baltic countries, and England. She added to that some $300 million which her importers didn't pay our exporters, and for which we made a loan to Brazil so she could pay our exporters, because they previously had spent our dollars.

That makes a deficit on Brazilian trade alone of $536 million of our dollars that they didn't use to buy goods in the United States. Talk about the dollar shortage! What I have to say about Brazil is also true in a lesser sense with every other country in South America.

Anti-American feeling is rife in South America. It is being fed by the Peronists and is being fed by the Communists. And they work together so closely that one can't tell them apart. The blank walls in South American cities and some of the walls of our embassies are lettered in tar, night after night: *"Go home, Nord Americano,"* or *"Leave our country Yanqui pigs."* Read the dispatches every day in the financial journals, from Bolivia, yesterday. Read the article in the *United States News* this week on the question-and-answer interview with the President of Bolivia, if you want to know what is happening to Americans in foreign countries.

Is Europe safe? I do not know any more than you what the Russian timetable may be; whether it is 1956 or some other date to occupy Europe. But I see nothing to stop Russia from marching into the Near East and taking Iran and Iraq and the Persian oil fields when it wants to. And when they do, they will infiltrate through Italy, on, of course, to North Africa, and the Mediterranean will become a Russian lake, and Gibraltar, flying the British flag, will become a mockery at the pillars of Hercules.

What are we going to do about it? Are we going to go to work together collectively to uphold America, or do we tear ourselves apart with our respective strife, decimating our strength? The last stand of capitalism in a diseased world becomes gradually weakened by the inability of its own segments of population to support a sound national policy.

Yes, our exports are falling off—diminuendo. We should now be exporting fifty million tons of coal from our shipping ports. It would be a great boon to our industry and mean more national income and more tax revenue for the government, more buying power for the people. But we are not exporting American coal because our government has no interest in trade. Apparently it doesn't go with striped pants and Homburg hats. And as a result Europe is getting its excess coal requirements for a rehabilitated (more or less) economy from behind the Iron Curtain.

What do they use for money? The Russians and the Poles won't take Italian lira; they won't take the French franc for their coal; they won't take the Dutch guilder; they won't take the pound sterling. They want American dollars. Rehabilitated Europe is buying Polish and Czechoslovakian coal with American dollars coming from American taxpayers, which has been concealed in some appropriation or some State Department method of bookkeeping. Conceivably, we could furnish Europe the coal and save our taxpayers the dollars. The coal industry has suggested it to the government. But they understand politics and they don't understand economics, I suppose.

Japan is a manufacturing nation of eighty-eight million people. We hope some day to abandon our garrisoning of that country—withdrawing our troops. Japan needs coal and she doesn't have any—not of a high-grade metallurgical quality. There is no reason why we shouldn't be keeping twenty Liberty ships constantly carrying cargoes of coal to Japan on a perfectly legitimate, open and shut, business-like arrangement that means a profit for everyone concerned. Now we furnish Japan with the dollars and Japan buys Manchurian coal with little financing.

That is something else we have not arranged. We have an investment here. We have the capital in the industry. Our railroads have the equipment to transport it. We have the ships to send it overseas. We have the men who want the employment. We have a government that wants the tax revenue. Why, in the name of all that is common sense, don't we furnish Japan with coal instead of letting the Russians do it?

Those are the problems that are coming tomorrow in our country and they are coming apace. Those are problems that are not going to be adjusted in a day or a week or a year; those are continuing problems.

What is going to happen in the world fight against Communism? After a truce in Korea—if a truce comes in Korea—and after England moves for the admission of Red China into the world organization and when—and after our statesmen protest—China is permitted to enter the world organization. It is plain to see now that England, our ally, is going to force the admission of Red China into the security council and other adjuncts of that organization as a quid pro quo for permitting an armistice to be brought about in Korea. Our statesmen know it; it is evident that they know it in their lack of emphasis about what they are going to do about it. That's the way England plays. That's the way England has ever played on every page of history that you can turn over since the Battle of Hastings. And when England makes common cause with Russia, what do we Americans do?

I suggest that we'd better counsel together and work together and forget that sometimes evident desire to annihilate each other, or we're going to awaken and find that we not only have profound and serious economic questions to face, but questions of world politics and relationships that run to the very preservation of modern civilization.

There are not only the moral values which are at stake; there are the social and economic values and the material considerations of life and the destiny, under our flag, of our sons and daughters who will follow us.

COMPETITION—LIFEBLOOD OF AMERICAN CAPITALISM [9]

Eric Johnston [10]

Eric Johnston, president of the Motion Picture Association of America, gave this address as one of the Community Lecture Series, at Jackson, Michigan, Tuesday evening, September 29, 1953.

The ideas of this speech were typical of Johnston's economic philosophy. His was a stand on hard and fast "competition," the integrity of private enterprise as basic to American economic health and progress. His position, however, was not that of unmitigated Adam Smith economics, but rather that of the middle-of-the-ground regulated American enterprise of the mid-twentieth century. Johnston would limit capitalistic monopoly and the undirected production and distribution of goods. Thus he would condemn both economic Nazi-Communist statism and socialism (full fledged or modified). Critics of his assumptions would reexamine the practicability and success of America's intermediate policy with regard to antitrust legislation and our record of public power developments and controls. Johnston's view of America's international trade aims and possible attainments would be especially open to sharp debate. How was the lowering of our tariff barriers to be practically achieved? And how could the various trade barriers within free Europe and between Europe and this country be minimized? And what were we to do about Soviet economic penetration?

Johnston, usually clever, interesting, personal, and even semi-slangy, was at Jackson more formal and perhaps more thoughtful. But his skill in audience adjustment and conciliation, his use of concrete and plausible evidence and illustration were still marks of his personal mode of communication. He continued to be an extempore speaker, pleasing in voice quality and rate control, and lively in his communication. [11]

Because I regard competition in commerce and industry as a force so crucial in our lives that it might decisively determine the course of the human race, I would like to discuss it with you this evening.

---

[9] Text supplied, and permission for this reprinting, through the courtesy of Eric Johnston and Kenneth Clark, vice president of the Motion Picture Association of America.

[10] For biographical note, see Appendix.

[11] For further comment on Eric Johnston as speaker, and examples of his speeches, see *Representative American Speeches: 1943-44*, p200-8; *1944-45*, p 175-85; *1950-51*, p 112-16.

It is to competition more than anything else that we in America owe our unparalleled standard of living and our unmatched proficiency in production and distribution.

Now it may sound strange coming from a member of an industry that has been hard hit by it, but I attribute our competitive economy, with all its benefits to producer and consumer alike, to our antitrust legislation. This charter of American economic rights is entitled to take its place, along with the Magna Charta, on the road to freedom as a monumental milepost.

That's a controversial statement and I know I am not going to get away with it unchallenged. I am prepared to back it up.

Societies that shun competition as the practice of knaves violating the rules of the club sometimes try to explain away our form of economy by ascribing it to geographic good fortune and lucky accident.

They argue that the new world naturally bred rivalry with its gold rushes and Sooner races—that opening up new territory and pushing back frontiers just had to lead to competition.

With some justice they will remind us that we enjoy a free and common market that sprung from unity, not rivalry, that our original colonies banded together primarily for military and political reasons and that the concept of a common market was secondary, if it existed at all.

To a point, but to a point only, these explanations have validity. Beyond that point, they are not explanations, but alibis. After all, we had our oldtime robber barons who tried to kill off competition and whack up the loot among themselves.

Moreover, physical expansion reached its limits many years ago. We could have fallen on old and evil habits. We could have settled down to a restricted economy complete with protective barriers and captive markets—but we didn't.

At the historic crossroads, our society faced up to its destiny and made the fateful decision which marked us as the world leaders of the future and the champions of modern capitalism.

We pushed through antitrust legislation which thenceforth outlawed collusion among producers to fix prices and rig markets at the expense of the buying public. It gave the little independent a chance to stand on his own feet and offer competition to the advantage of the consumer. These laws were no accident of history, no blessing of geography.

True like any other laws, antitrust legislation has been violated and even misapplied on more than one occasion, but in the long run these measures guarantee that the lifeblood of modern capitalism—competition—will not be drained off by the greedy or the short-sighted.

This decisive step, it seems to me, has been primarily responsible for the flowering of an economy that makes us substantially different from other societies. There is a distinction that needs strong underscoring.

When we talk about two worlds nowadays, we generally have in mind the two major opposing camps of our times—the free world and the Communist bloc. We blandly assume that those of us who are bound together by common political objectives likewise share mutual economic principles. We don't.

This difference which exists between America and most of her allies does not lend itself readily to drama and headlines. It is not the colorful subject of diplomatic maneuvers and dashing communiques and because it isn't, it tends to get lost in the shuffle of events that beset our lives.

Yet this difference is of critical importance, for it is the cause of a fundamental split in the free world approach to the problems of the day. United though we may be in our opposition to communistic imperialism, the capitalistic democracies are severely handicapped in launching a joint offensive of substantial effectiveness as long as this economic chasm exists.

Let us take a look at capitalism as it works in the United States and see where it differs from capitalism abroad.

Competition has kept our producers on their toes to the delight of the buying public. Most of them realize the futility of conspiring among themselves. They do not try to crush or freeze out their rivals. Instead they seek to outdo each other in technical advances, and in advertising, merchandising, repair and replacement. American entrepreneurs plow an ever mounting percentage of their profits back into their business to improve their products, for they know that the consumer is the final judge. In our economy the slogan "The Customer Is Always Right" has rich and real meaning.

Commercial rivalry is responsible for ever higher quality and better values in the products we turn out and the services we render. This is a continuing process which is growing, not slowing down. In spite of so-called cheap money, the American market today offers better buys than ever before, and there is every reason to believe that tomorrow will be an impovement over today.

It is a popular pastime these days to dwell on the glories of the old hard dollar when we allegedly could buy so much more for so much less. But think it over for a moment, was this really true?

The era of ten-cent milk was marked by the ten-dollar weekly wage as well. That was no bargain.

And even if your income was adequate then, what kind of an automobile could you get back in 1920, let us say, for six thousand old fashioned dollars? If it did sixty miles an hour downhill, it was a demon's vehicle. If it could go uphill without a change in gears, it was a powerhouse. And you could really brag about economy if you got twelve miles to a gallon of gas. Besides, was it very comfortable? Did it have style and beauty or any of the conveniences and safety factors we know today?

Why, with a third as many dollars now, you can get many times the automobile you could thirty years ago.

The story is the same in so many other products and services— radios, motion pictures, communications, are just some of them. It is competition that has stimulated our producers to dedicate themselves to serve the public on the grand and practical scale.

I am not implying that American businessmen are so lofty that they welcomed competition from the outset. Who ever does? Yet, faced with rivalry, our entrepreneurs have made the most of it. Indeed, they have improved because of it to a point where American management, production and salesmanship have few, if any, equals anywhere.

Now why should Americans enjoy virtually unchallenged industrial and commercial leadership in the modern world? Our country was not the mother of the Industrial Revolution. That honor belongs to Great Britain. We cannot lay undisputed claim to superior craftsmanship, nor do we have a monopoly on managerial brains.

The fundamental answer, it seems to me, is that our economy is sparked by competition and we thrive on expanding markets. In most other societies, the economy is restricted, production is rigged, prices are fixed and the markets are captive.

When consumer demand falls off in the United States, our producers make strenuous efforts to gain new customers and to hold old ones by cutting prices and by making products more attractive.

In other lands, the general practice is to match falling markets with curtailed production and maintained prices. Without competition there is a premium on scarcity. With it, the accent is on growing markets.

In the light of this important difference between capitalism as Americans know it and capitalism as it is practiced abroad, is it surprising to learn that American manufacturers, to keep up with their rivals, feel compelled to replace plant machinery on the average of once every four and a half years, while in France, for example, industrial equipment has a normal operating life of something like seventeen and a half years?

American specialists who surveyed British coal mines in 1940 were startled to discover that most of them were operating with equipment that had been installed as long ago as 1913. Little wonder then that the American coal miner outproduces his British counterpart by six to one, in spite of the six-hour day in American pits.

These are only two examples of how far ahead of most other people we are and how different our brand of capitalism is from theirs. In countries less advanced than Britain or France, the gap is even greater.

What is true in production is equally true in distribution, salesmanship and service. Proficiency in these fields is a condition for survival and success in the American business world. Elsewhere it is frowned upon.

In Europe, which has fewer states than we have, there is no free and common market. Imports are choked by protectionist restrictions and quotas. Exports are given an economic false-face by state subsidies.

In our country enlightened managers and forthright labor leaders have also played key roles in establishing the kind of buyers' economy we have today.

The pressure of rising wages has forced producers to expand their markets. As profits decreased on each unit through rising costs, the entrepreneur increased the volume of his sales to assure his undertaking of adequate returns.

Moreover, higher wages have also meant increased mass purchasing power—one very practical way of expanding markets. For a mass production society, it means mass consumption—without which such an economy could not flourish.

American products made under competitive conditions are in universal demand. The success of our motion pictures is typical of the impact of our products on the world market. Although many countries have movie industries of their own, our pictures occupy about 72 per cent of the playing time on the world's screens in the face of quotas and protective restrictions.

In many foreign lands it is considered fashionable these days to criticize American products. In some countries it is a hallmark of nationalism and patriotism to do so.

How often do we hear that our cars flash too much chrome, that we place too much accent on our bathrooms or that our movies portray too many cowboys?

It is my guess that there is some kind of a direct ratio between the volume of sales and the amount of talk about a product.

Coca Cola takes a pasting in Paris but its sales move up. On the other hand, it is easy to understand why astrakhan hats are not exactly the subject of daily conversation around the world—favorable or unfavorable. How many of us have ever seen one in the first place?

While taking pride in what we have done, we ought not to be smug about our achievements and our practices. We are not simon-pure especially when we are confronted with opposition from abroad. After all, international commerce is a **two-way** street. Our domestic market, we must remember, is someone else's foreign market.

If we are justified in criticizing other countries for throttling foreign trade through protectionism, we are also open to the charge that we are sometimes guilty of the same misdeed and with less justification.

We are not entitled to do any strutting—we have no right to champion competitive capitalism if we do not stand ready to take on all comers and accept all challenges no matter whence they come.

Even though foreign entrepreneurs have the benefit of cheaper labor, we have competed successfully with them, because of our greater efficiency and our willingness to invest in progress. The most dangerous competitor any American producer has is another American producer.

I would like to see the American businessman get protection from cheap labor products by seeing wages go up abroad, not by seeing tariffs go up at home.

If we cast the economic mote out of our own eye, our criticism of others would serve a better purpose. We could then without embarrassment urge other capitalistic societies to launch reforms and to abandon protectionism. As leaders, is it not our duty to set the example, if we want others to follow? Our suggestions will more likely be heeded if we practice for ourselves what we preach for others.

Cooperation, it seems to me, consists of roughly equal parts of operating and "co-ing." The Western world proved long ago that it knows how to operate. It has mastered the sciences and the crafts. But the time has come when the rest of the free world, and especially free Europe, must meet the challenge that confronts it. It must abandon monopoly capitalism and go competitive.

It must strive for free and common markets by knocking down barriers and restrictions. It must call a halt to protectionism which rewards the inadequate at the expense of the public. Its producers must look for their profits in expanding sales, not in fixed prices and captive markets.

In twentieth century society, governments must meet the demands of the people and free enterprise must meet their needs. If they fail, the police state will follow and then people will meet the demands of government and enterprise will serve the needs of the commissars.

It is not enough to dig a foxhole against communism. Our way of life depends on an expanding economy, on growing markets, and we must do what we can to encourage their growth throughout the world.

Surely, one way to do this is to sponsor programs which will open up the channels of international trade, and give free reign to competition among nations and among industries within nations.

The incompetent and the inadequate may suffer under such a system, but we know that the buying public will gain.

There is no justification for giving protection, public or private, to anyone in any field who shirks service to the public.

It would be unrealistic to think that tomorrow we will induce the rest of the world to discard practices that have become entrenched over the years, but if we can't teach an old dog new tricks, there is a chance at least that we might succeed in preventing a new dog from learning old tricks.

New industries are opening up and expanding. Plastics, atomic energy and agricultural chemistry are just a few of them. We must do what we can to see that such new undertakings spread and grow—that they get off to a healthy start. We ought not be a party to any new cartels. Instead we ought to give the old ones a dose of medicine that will cure or kill them—competition. After all, it is difficult to be a spoiled child in a large family.

When capitalism stops expanding, it begins to die. Monopoly capitalism is an old and tired system, incapable of growth and unable to meet the daily needs of people.

It would be a tragic error to assume that it is the friend of our way of life. It is an enemy of progress and expansion, and for that reason, it inadvertently helps the cause of communism.

If the free world is to triumph in the end, it must think in terms of new horizons, not old frontiers. It cannot march forward under one political banner and be split down the middle economically.

One of our foremost problems today is this difference in economic concept between America and so many of her allies. The solution of that problem, the healing of that split, ought to get the highest kind of priority. It is the only way we can muster the combined strength of the free world partners in sufficient force to stem the tide of Communist imperialism.

Unless we close ranks by opening up our economies—by opening them up to the people—we shall be disastrously weakened in our efforts to stand up to the world-wide threat of Kremlin domination.

It is our task, our mission, our destiny, if you please, to translate human wants into demands and demands into consumption.

We are doing this now in the United States. It must be done everywhere—and it can be, if the producers of the free world meet their responsibilities to history by serving the public. Dedicated to that aim, they will not have to fear competition, nor cry for protection.

If variety is the spice of life, then competition is the spice of variety. Surely, it is the spice of our economy and of our way of life, and so it must be for the rest of the civilized world if the values we treasure and the bounties we enjoy are to endure.

INTELLECTUAL AND RELIGIOUS IDEALS

THE LIBERAL ARTS IN CONTEMPORARY
AMERICAN SOCIETY [1]

GEORGE F. KENNAN [2]

George F. Kennan, former ambassador to Russia, gave this address at Notre Dame University, South Bend, Indiana, on May 15, 1953. His was the principal address at a special convocation marking the dedication of the I. A. O'Shaughnessy Hall of Liberal and Fine Arts, a $2,300,000 building donated by Mr. O'Shaughnessy. This new home of liberal arts was to house the oldest of the five colleges. The award of an honorary degree to Mr. Kennan was part of the program.

The speaker's thesis was that "forces at large in our society march in one way or another under the banner of an alarmed and exercised anticommunism." They "incorrectly state the problem" and find the wrong answers—namely in their breeding of timidity, fear, and suspicion.

Though Kennan talked in general terms of the contemporary anti-communism activities and attitudes, he and his audience as he spoke were no doubt pin-pointing each indictment with much concrete illustration. The press, radio, and television each day were unfolding the methods of the investigative committees that the speaker was denouncing.

Kennan has had long and close experience with communism and Sovietism. For some twenty-six years since his graduation from Princeton, he has filled various diplomatic posts in Berlin, Moscow, and elsewhere in Europe. He has also served on the policy-planning staff of the Department of State and been adviser to the Secretary of State on European Affairs. President Truman appointed him ambassador to Russia in 1952, but not long afterward that nation declared him unacceptable. He subsequently resigned the diplomatic service and returned to the Institute for Advanced Study at Princeton. He was the author of the famous article in *Foreign Affairs* in 1947 in which "Mr. X" advocated a policy of "containment" of Russia. His record was thus one of vigorous opposition to the Kremlin ideologies.

Not a vigorous public speaker, shy, scholarly, he nevertheless spoke at Notre Dame with a warmth and decisiveness of phrase that caused wide comment and brought strong endorsement from the advocates of liberalism in this country.

[1] Text and permission for this reprint supplied through the courtesy of the author.

[2] For biographical note, see Appendix.

I find it difficult to begin these remarks without telling you how much it means to me to be here, in my native Middle West, and yet in just such a setting and for just such an occasion. One is always sensitive about one's native region, as one is about one's own family; and in the return to it one looks at it with eyes at once eagerly wistful and ruthlessly critical.

Nothing—I think—could be more warming and reassuring for the returning native son than the sight of this campus and the nature of this occasion. Cardinal Newman once said: "A university . . . is a place which wins the admiration of the young by its celebrity, kindles the affections of the middle aged by its beauty, and rivets the fidelity of the old by its associations." This observation causes me to feel today that I must be both young and old; because when I see this university and sense its life and spirit, I experience both the admiration and affection which Newman mentioned, and I understand well the bond of fidelity which such an institution creates in its own sons.

The sense of warmth and reassurance that flows from this occasion means all the more to me because I cannot forget that there are forces at large in our society today that do not inspire me with this same feeling—quite the contrary. These forces are too diffuse to be described by their association with the name of any one man or any one political concept. They have no distinct organizational forms. They are as yet largely matters of the mind and the emotion in large masses of individuals. But they all march, in one way or another, under the banner of an alarmed and exercised anticommunism—but an anticommunism of a quite special variety, bearing an air of excited discovery and proprietorship, as though no one had ever known before that there was a Communist danger, as though no one had ever thought about it and taken its measure, as though it had all begun about the year 1945 and these people were the first to learn of it.

I have no quarrel to pick with the ostensible purposes of the people in whom these forces are manifest. Surely, many of them are sincere. Surely, many of them are good people. Surely, many of them have come to these views under real provocation and out of real bewilderment. But I have the deepest misgivings about the direction and effects of their efforts. In general, I feel that what they are doing is unwise and unfortunate, and I am against it. They distort and exaggerate the dimensions of the problem with which they profess to deal. They confuse internal and external aspects of the Communist threat. They insist on portraying as contemporary realities things that had their actuality years ago. They insist on ascribing to the workings of domestic communism evils and frustrations which, in so far as they were not part of the normal and unavoidable burden of complexity in our life, were the product of our behavior generally as a nation, and should today be the subject of humble and contrite soul-searching on the part of all of us, in a spirit of brotherhood and community, rather than of frantic and bitter recrimination. And having thus incorrectly stated the problem, it is no wonder that these people consistently find the wrong answers. They tell us to remove our eyes from the constructive and positive purposes and to pursue with fanaticism the negative and vindictive ones. They sow timidity where there should be boldness; fear where there should be serenity; suspicion where there should be confidence and generosity. In this way they impel us—in the name of our salvation from the dangers of communism—to many of the habits of thought and action which our Soviet adversaries, I am sure, would most like to see us adopt and which they have tried unsuccessfully over a period of some thirty-five years to graft upon us through the operations of their Communist party.

I would not mention these things if I felt that they were only my personal concern and had no relation to the undertaking which we have gathered today to celebrate. But I fear that there is here a serious relevance which we cannot ignore.

Thanks to the vision of wise and generous people, this university is now adding one more important unit to the number of those facilities in our country in which men can cultivate their own understanding, and extend the boundaries of knowledge, in the fields of arts and letters. Certainly there could be no finer undertaking, and none more needed. But I feel that this undertaking, too, will have to deal at some point with the forces I have just described—that by entering upon this undertaking you will eventually find that these forces will be your concern just as they have already become the concern of some of us who have walked in other paths of life.

I feel this first of all because these forces are narrowly exclusive in their approach to our world position, and carry this exclusiveness vigorously into the field of international cultural exchanges. They tend to stifle the interchange of cultural impulses that is vital to the progress of the intellectual and artistic life of our people. The people in question seem to feel either that cultural values are not important at all or that America has reached the apex of cultural achievement and no longer needs in any serious way the stimulus of normal contact with other peoples in the field of arts and letters. They look with suspicion both on the sources of intellectual and artistic activity in this country and on impulses of this nature coming to us from abroad. The remote pasts of foreign artists and scholars are anxiously scanned before they are permitted to enter our land, and this is done in proceedings so inflexible in concept and offensive in execution that their very existence often constitutes a discouragement to cultural interchange. The personal movements and affairs of great scholars and artists are thus passed upon and controlled by people who have no inkling of understanding for the creative work these same scholars and artists perform. In this way, we begin to draw about ourselves a cultural curtain similar in some respects to the Iron Curtain of our adversaries. In doing so, we tend to inflict upon ourselves a species of cultural isolation and provincialism wholly out of accord with the traditions of our nation and destined, if unchecked, to bring to our intellectual and artistic life the same sort of sterility from which the cultural world of our Communist adversaries is already suffering.

A second reason why I think you will have to concern yourselves with the forces to which I have pointed is that within the framework of our society, as in its relations to external environment, the tendency of these forces is exclusive and intolerant—quick to reject, slow to receive, intent on discovering what ought *not* to be rather than what *ought* to be. They claim the right to define a certain area of our national life and cultural output as beyond the bounds of righteous approval. This definition is never effected by law or by constituted authority; it is effected by vague insinuation and suggestion. And the circle tends to grow constantly narrower. One has the impression that if uncountered, these people would eventually reduce the area of political and cultural respectability to a point where it included only themselves, the excited accusers, and excluded everything and everybody not embraced in the profession of denunciation.

I recall reading recently, twice in one day, the words of individuals who proclaimed that if certain other people did not get up and join actively in the denunciation of Communists or communism, they would thereby themselves be suspect. What sort of arrogance is this? Every one of us has his civic obligations. Every one of us has his moral obligations to the principles of loyalty and decency. I am not condoning any one for forgetting these obligations. But to go beyond this—say that it is not enough to be a law-abiding citizen—to say that we all have some obligation to get up and make statements of this tenor or that with respect to other individuals, or else submit to being classified as suspect in the eyes of our fellow citizens—to assert this is to establish a new species of public ritual, to arrogate to one's individual self the powers of the spiritual and temporal law-giver, to make the definition of social conduct a matter of fear in the face of vague and irregular forces, rather than a matter of confidence in the protecting discipline of conscience and the law.

I would know of no moral or political authority for this sort of thing. I tremble when I see this attempt to make a semi-religious cult out of emotional political currents of the moment, and particularly when I note that these currents are ones exclusively negative in nature, designed to appeal only to men's capacity for hatred and fear, never to their capacity for forgiveness and charity and understanding. I have lived more than ten years of my life in totalitarian countries. I know where this sort of thing leads. I know it to be the most shocking and cynical disservice one can do to the credulity and to the spiritual equilibrium of one's fellowmen.

And this sort of thing cannot fail to have its effect on the liberal arts, for it is associated with two things that stand in deepest conflict to the development of mind and spirit: with a crass materialism and anti-intellectualism on the one hand, and with a marked tendency toward standardization and conformity on the other.

In these forces I have spoken about, it seems to me that I detect a conscious rejection and ridicule of intellectual effort and distinction. They come together here with a deep-seated weakness in the American character: a certain shy self-consciousness that tends to deny interests other than those of business, sport, or war. There is a powerful strain of our American cast of mind that has little use for the artist or the writer, and professes to see in the pursuits of such people a lack of virility —as though virility could not find expression in the creation of beauty, as though Michaelangelo had never wielded his brush, as though Dante had never taken up his pen, as though the plays of Shakespeare were lacking in manliness. The bearers of this neo-materialism seem, indeed, to have a strange self-consciousness about the subject of virility—a strange need to emphasize and demonstrate it by exhibitions of taciturnity, callousness, and physical aggressiveness—as though there were some anxiety lest, in the absence of these exhibitions, it might be found wanting. What weakness is it in us Americans that so often makes us embarrassed or afraid to indulge the gentle impulse, to seek the finer and rarer flavor, to admit frankly and without stammering apologies to an appreciation for the wonder of the poet's word and the miracle of the artist's brush, for all the beauty, in short, that has been recorded in the images of word and line created by the hands of men in past ages? What is it that makes us fear to acknowledge the greatness of other lands, or of other times, to shun the subtle and the unfamiliar? What is it that causes us to huddle together, herdlike, in tastes and enthusiasms that represent only the common denominator of popular acquiescence rather than to show ourselves receptive to the tremendous flights of creative imagination of which the individual mind has shown itself capable? Is it that we are forgetful of the true sources of our moral strength, afraid of ourselves, afraid to look into the chaos of our own breasts, afraid of the bright, penetrating light of the great teachers?

This fear of the untypical, this quest for security within the walls of secular uniformity—these are traits of our national character we would do well to beware of and to examine for their origins. They receive much encouragement these days, much automatic and unintended encouragement, by virtue of the growing standardization of the cultural and, in many respects, the educational influences to which our people are being subjected. The immense impact of commercial advertising and the mass media on our lives is—let us make no mistake about it—an impact that tends to encourage passivity, to encourage acquiescence and uniformity, to place handicaps on individual contemplativeness and creativeness.

It may not seem to many of us too dangerous that we should all live, dress, eat, hear, and read substantially alike. But we forget how easily this uniformity of thought and habit can be exploited, when the will to exploit it is there. We forget how easily it can slip over into domination of our spiritual and political lives by self-appointed custodians who contrive to set themselves at the head of popular emotional currents.

There is a real and urgent danger here for anyone who values the right to differ from others in any manner whatsoever, be it in his interests or his associations or his faith. There is no greater mistake we of this generation can make than to imagine that the tendencies which in other countries have led to the nightmare of totalitarianism will, as they appear in our own midst, politely pause—out of some delicate respect for American tradition—at the point where they would begin to affect our independence of mind and belief. The forces of intolerance and political demagoguery are greedy forces, and unrestrained. There is no limit to their ambitions or their impudence. They contain within themselves no mechanism of self-control. Like the ills of Pandora's box, once released, they can be stopped only by forces external to themselves.

It is for these reasons that I feel that you, in setting up at this time within this great academic community a center for liberal arts, are taking upon yourselves a great, though honorable, burden. You are going to have to swim against the tide of many of the things I have been talking about. You are frequently going to find arrayed against you, whether by intent or otherwise, the materialists, the anti-intellectuals, the chauvinists of all sizes and descriptions, the protagonists of violence and suspicion and intolerance, the people who take it upon themselves to delimit the operation of the principle of Christian charity, the people from whose memories there has passed the recollection that in their Father's house there are many mansions. What you do in these walls will often be unsettling and displeasing to such people. They will view it with jealousy. You will have to bear their malice and their misrepresentation. But, unlike what many of them profess to wish to do to their own chosen enemies, it will be your task not to destroy them but to help in their redemption and remaking, to open their eyes, to demonstrate to them the sterility and hopelessness of negative undertakings, to engender in them an awareness of the real glories and the real horizons of the human spirit.

In this lies both the duty and the opportunity of the devotees of the liberal arts within our contemporary American civilization. It lies with them to combat the standardization of our day: to teach people to accept the great richness of the human mind and fantasy—to welcome it and to rejoice in it, happy that we have not been condemned by nature to a joyless monotony of the creative faculty, happy that there are so many marvelous ways in which the longings and dreams of men can find expression. It lies with the devotees of the liberal arts to combat the materialism of our time: to teach us how to ride to work in a motor vehicle and absorb the canned music of the advertisers without forgetting that there is also a music of the spheres, to force us to remember that all the manifestations of our material prowess, impressive as they seem, are nevertheless only impermanent auxiliaries to our existence—that the only permanent thing behind them all is still the naked, vulnerable, human soul, the scene of the age-old battle between good and evil, assailed with weakness and imperfections, always in need of help and support, and yet sometimes capable of such breath-taking impulses of faith and creative imagination.

Finally, it lies with the devotees of the liberal arts to combat the forces of intolerance in our society: to convince people that these forces are incompatible with the flowering of the human spirit, to remember that the ultimate judgments of good and evil are not ours to make: that the wrath of man against his fellow man must always be tempered by the recollection of his weakness and fallibility and by the example of forgiveness and redemption which is the essence of his Christian heritage.

I have tried to give you in these words a picture of the role of the liberal arts institution as I see it, and of its relation to the problems of our American civilization at this time. I assign to it in my thoughts, as you see, a duty and a function that could hardly be more important. To those of you who are going to participate in the direction of this institution, and to those who are going to work within its sheltering and inspiring walls, I can only say that you have the deepest good wishes and the bated hopes of all of us who wish to see preserved the great qualities by which this nation has thus far been distinguished: its tolerance, its good nature, its decency, its health of spirit. May your accomplishments be worthy of your opportunities. May they give fruition to the excellent impulses that have made possible this beginning.

ALIVE [3]

Louis H. Evans [4]

Dr. Louis H. Evans gave this sermon at the Easter Sunrise Service in the Hollywood Bowl, California, April 5, 1953. This discourse, like many others by Dr. Evans, was broadcast over KFWB, Hollywood. For twelve years he was head minister of the First Presbyterian Church, in Hollywood, with more than six thousand communicants, "the largest Presbyterian church congregation in America." Dr. Evans resigned his Hollywood pastorate, as of May 1, 1953, to become minister-at-large for the National Board of the Presbyterian Church, U.S.A.

The sermon was typical of this clergyman's homiletic method. (1) The opening quotation served as a text. (2) The Easter theme of the resurrected life was illustrated by numerous biblical citations, by the quotation from a poem, and by a brief anecdote. (3) The construction followed a simple pattern, easily remembered: (a) purposes in life, (b) pardon, and (c) a program. (4) The introduction was swift and the concluding sections a direct application to his immediate and his radio listeners. (5) The language, without academic or complicated phrasing, was readily comprehensible to thousands who might listen. (6) Rhetorical questions were used. (7) The emotional mood was dominant ("the crimson sacrifice that can add to the color of the dawning of His freedom for all mankind"), but rhetorical exuberance and studied originality were almost absent. (8) The note was personally evangelical, rather than strongly social, but expressed in the philosophy of a conservative Presbyterian.

Dr. Evans is strong in delivery, with a record of many years of pulpit effectiveness. Physically he is more than six feet tall and suggests a college athlete. His voice is well trained (one of his instructors was A. E. Phillips, of Chicago, widely famed as a teacher of public speaking). His tones are deep, well modulated, and his radio transmission especially effective. Typical of his vocal manner is his frequent use of the dramatic pause. In the pulpit he is often relaxed, crossing his arms, or casually leaning on the lectern. His speech is General American.[5]

This Christ of Easter came saying: "I am come that ye might have life." Did He mean to infer that those persons who

[3] Text furnished through the courtesy of Dr. Louis H. Evans, with his permission for this reprint.

[4] For biographical note, see Appendix.

[5] This editor is indebted to Mrs. Anna Kerr, a graduate student at the University of Southern California, for her study of "The Sermonic Discourses of Louis Hadley Evans."

heard him that day were not living? Is it not arresting that everyone that breathes does not really live? A blacksmith's bellows breathes but it does not live!

Life—real spiritual life—of which the rock, the tree, the grape, the bird, the ox know nothing—is made up of certain living things which are the gift of God. They are found splendidly in Easter.

Easter reminds us first of all of the necessity of a *purpose in life.* It is quite possible for a thing to move and not know where it is going. It is possible to have power but no purpose; to have speed but no direction. Sometimes we play games with no goals and build houses that somehow never become homes because love is not there. It is possible to exist and never know how the purpose for which we were created—to "Seek first the Kingdom of God and its righteousness." Christ said, "For this cause came I into the world" and no friends ever laid to rest the body of a man so alive to why He was here.

Easter offers us *pardon.* There are two kinds of "death." There is that physical death that takes place when the soul is separated from the body. This none of us can escape. Then there is that spiritual death that takes place when the soul is separated from God by unforgiven sin. He who can remove that sin and bring God and man together again can restore life. This Christ came to do—"once in the end of the age hath He appeared to put away sin by the sacrifice of Himself in His death." When men contested that this forgiveness of sins was the prerogative of God and asked for proof of His ability to do this, he replied "Destroy this body and in three days God will raise it again. My resurrection will be God's stamp and imprimatur on my saviorship.' He rose and thus sin could be removed between God and man until man found that sin which separated and made him at enmity with God was now dissolved and now God and man could be "at one" in this thrilling "at-one-ment"— "Atonement" which Easter verified. Now men can cry "My sins, O the bliss of that glorious thought, my sin not in part but the whole, is nailed to the cross and I bear it no more, praise the

Lord, O my soul." Without this pardon Easter loses much of its significance.

Easter also assures us of a *program*. Christ invited us to pray this brave prayer and accept this great program, "Thy Kingdom come, Thy will be done on earth as it is in heaven." Is there any use in embracing that magnificent purpose? Could God's will ever be done on earth as it is in heaven?

Were Christ's three years of public ministry on earth a prophecy of what He could do through the ages to come? Would this sort of power stay with them? Could He who changed the wild man of Gadara into his right mind do this for the fevered spirit of nations? Could He who stilled the Galilean Sea still the heart of humanity and the cosmos? Could He who told the lame man to rise and walk heal a war-torn maimed world. Is He so truly the Prince of Peace? As He wooed a drunkard from his cup, could He make a community sober? If He could take Mary Magdalene and turn her from "mud to stars" could He do that for all mankind?

Men never saw God so clearly at work as during those three years before the tomb. Now He was to die—would that be the end of all this magnificence? They had seen philosophers at work before but not this force of life-changing power. This was it. Now would death end it all?

Then Christ in answer laid down the issue. "Destroy this body and in three days God will raise it again. I risk everything at one throw. If I do not rise from the dead it is the end of what I am and what I brought to you. If I do rise then swing behind me and wager everything at one throw. If I do not rise from the dead it is the end of what I am and what I brought to you. If I do rise then swing behind me and wager everything on me. I will have my third day!"

> And sitting down, they watched Him there,
> The soldiers did;
> There, while they played with dice,
> He made his sacrifice,
> And died upon the Cross to rid
> God's world of sin.

> He was a gambler, too, my Christ,
> He took His life and threw
> It for a world redeemed
> And ere His agony was done,
> Before the westering sun went down,
> Crowning that day with crimson crown,
> He knew that He had won.
>   —G. A. STUDDERT-KENNEDY

He had his third day! He arose at dawning and as Christ was imperishable and eternal so are the things He brought to us— recuperation, regeneration, redemption, change, pardon, renewal, victory. Those things, thank God, are as indestructible as is He. "He is alive—the tomb is empty." It spread like a prairie fire over land and sea. His program, His pardon and His power are alive forevermore and are the eternal gifts to all who want them.

But will His Kingdom be unending—will it arise surely? As sure as the sun came up this morning—you knew it would— for it is God's sun. And His kingdom will rise because this is God's world. "This is my Father's world, the battle is not done; Jesus who died shall be satisfied and heaven and earth be one." This sound of dropping iron curtains to keep the church out, this shutting of doors to keep Christianity out is but the noise of the death rattle of agnosticism. Wait and see!

Have no fear for His church—the gates of hell shall not prevail against her. A store owner, standing amid the ruins of his burned-down establishment in the great Chicago fire posted a sign that read "Business as usual tomorrow morning." And the church will be there tomorrow morning. Many have prophesied her funeral but no one ever buries her—no one ever will.

Have no fear for Christian democracy in the end. It is not going to perish. And if you soldier, sailor or flier should spill your blood on Korean field or sea—believe that it could be but the crimson sacrifice that can add to the color of the dawning of His freedom for all mankind and say to Christ, "Lord, you and I helped the morning break in the realm of governance."

When loved ones are called by death remember there is a great tomorrow. If they are with Him and He is alive—so are they. Trust Him for that.

Remember those Christian standards men scoffed at are worth holding. They are as right and enduring as the stars.

This Easter experience can become real to you today and you, too, can "be raised to walk with Him in newness of life." You can personally walk out of the tomb and sarcophagus of your secular, defeated living; you can drop the habits that bind you round and round as graveclothes; the napkin of doubt can fall from your head and you can believe; as a caterpillar leaves its cocoon and with wings flies in the sky blue yonder so you need not always drag along worm-like, despondent, earthy and secular. As the Easter lily blooms white out of the mud so you can be better than the community in which you live.

The sun of a new life for you can rise as surely as this sun this morning.

This Bowl Service today is a salute to Christ and the undying things of Easter. So we have made our way to this hilltop at dawning simply to say to a world not awake or fully alive to life—"we have Christ. He is alive. And we live!"

May none of us miss this glorious boon and blessing of Easter morning.

CONVERTING LIABILITIES INTO ASSETS [6]

LOUIS L. MANN [7]

Dr. Louis L. Mann, rabbi of Sinai Congregation, Chicago, Illinois, gave this sermon before the Chicago Sunday Evening Club, Chicago, Illinois, on May 31, 1953. The address was also broadcast over station WIND, Chicago.

The Sunday Evening Club has had religious services in downtown Orchestra Hall since 1907, with the nation's leading preachers as guest speakers.

Rabbi Mann, who received his rabbinical training at Hebrew Union College, Cincinnati, also earned a doctorate of philosophy at Cornell University in 1920. Since 1924 he has been a member of the faculty of the University of Chicago, a lecturer on Oriental Languages.

He is both scholarly and popular in his public addresses. The present discourse was obviously adapted to both his immediate audience and to the mass radio listeners. This sermon is made up almost entirely of illustrations. Each is developed with concrete and vivid detail that give dramatic value to the central theme. The talk is thus purely inspirational rather than exegetical or doctrinal.

I have chosen as my subject tonight, "Converting Liabilities into Assets.' I think I could state my theme in the form of a paradox. *The greatest asset is to have a liability.* The greatest liability is to have no liability. A very interesting book appeared some time ago written by eleven psychiatrists who had locked themselves up together in a hotel for about a week to discuss a very important problem, "Why Men Fail." They came out with a dozen conclusions—some four or five of which I'll share with you this evening. The first is, that the *majority* of people who succeed in life are not more gifted than those who fail. Second: the majority of those who fail in life are not less gifted than those who succeed. Third: the majority of people go all through life using less than 40 per cent of their God-given abilities. That's like an eight-cylinder car chugging and jerking along on three cylinders. Four: the majority of people who have handicaps,

[6] Text furnished through the courtesy of Dr. Louis Mann, with permission for this reprint.

[7] For biographical note, see Appendix.

liabilities and frustrations, who are crippled or blind or deaf, who have every reason to fail—now mark you—the majority who have every reason to fail—fail to fail. They make good.

The *one* greatest cause for human failure is an alibi. An alibi is "personal enemy number one." An alibi is not a mere excuse for failure, but a rationalization which means a ready excuse, a plausible excuse, a well sounding excuse, which one hugs so tightly that one will not let it go and hence will find occasion to use it.

I can illustrate what I have in mind by referring to some very familiar biographies. I choose familiar ones because I believe they will drive my point home so much the better. During the last war I happened to have done some psychological reconditioning for the government at Gardner Hospital in Chicago. I dealt with young men and young women who had come home from struggle crippled and maimed as well as with mental problems of various kinds. I came across two people—strangely enough how things will happen—near whom one and the same shrapnel burst and amputated the right arm of each of these men. One of them said to me as I was making my rounds, "I'll sit back and take it easy and get $107 a month as long as I live; I can sit on the cracker barrel and be a philosopher." The other man heard him and he shook his left arm at me and he said, "Nothing will stop me. I'm going right ahead as if nothing had happened." This leads me to the conclusion which is part of my theme this evening: *what happens to us is less significant than what happens within us.*

I'm going to divide what I have to say in four parts; the first, I'm going to call Frustrations. I take my first example from the Bible. There was a prophet whose name was Hosea. He had a great liability; his wife went wrong. She was unfaithful and as happened in ancient times, she was taken down to the market place to be sold at auction to the highest bidder. Hosea wanted to be a thousand miles from that place that day, but somehow or other when the time for the auction came and people went to the market place; he found himself in the procession and then in the front row and strangely enough he became the highest bidder. She was his, not for a wife, but to take her back home to save her from greater degradation and shame. During the weeks and months that intervened, there came over him little by little a sense of forgiveness, and overwhelming pity seized his heart and a spiritual love emanated from his whole being; then it dawned upon him if a mere humble creature, like himself could so forgive and so love, how much greater must be the love of God for all of his unfortunate creatures. So, 740 years before Jesus, Hosea converted a liability into an imperishable asset and taught the world its greatest idea—*God is Love.*

Some years ago I visited Westminster Abbey where lie buried the immortals of the British empire. I walked around and saw some of the little slabs in the walls not more than nine inches wide. I recognized many of my book friends and as I passed one of those slabs, the shivers ran up and down my spine. Did that ever happen to you? It brought a story to my mind. He was a man whom I sympathetically called one of nature's stepchildren. He was born a hunchback and lame; he was a cripple, deformed and could hardly stand on his feet. He knew that nature had enslaved him. As he thought his problem through, an idea came to him: there are slaves whom nature has not enslaved, but whom man's inhumanity to man had enslaved. So he gave his whole life to freeing the enslaved. Once he was to make a speech; nobody could see him; they picked him up off the floor and put him upon the desk so that he could be seen. That night Boswell, the biographer of Johnson, was in the audience. When he left he said, "I saw them put a little shrimp on the table, but before he got through, he was a whale." Who was the "little shrimp" they put on the table and got to be "a whale"? It made my spine tingle. William Wilberforce. More than any one man in the entire British empire in its entire history he had freed the black man from bondage. On that little slab, were these imperishable words: "William Wilberforce, the attorney general for the unprotected and the friendless." The *attorney general for the unprotected and the friendless.* Frustrations!

What about the handicaps? I am thinking for the moment of a man named Whistler. The great ambition of his life was to be a soldier. He got an appointment and he went to West Point. At the end of the first year, to use the language of the streets, he "flunked' his chemistry. He was allowed to come back and the next year, he flunked his chemistry again and they had to drop him. He went back home. Some people go on a drunk when such things happen to them. They lose their courage in life, they feel they are no good, they are "washed out," they're done. He began scratching in the sand and he found that he could draw things. Then he began taking up colors and found out that he could mix colors and paint. I needn't tell you that Whistler became one of the great artists of all times. Now some of you are going to tell me he achieved fame *in spite* of his handicap and I say to you, *because* of his handicap. Later on in life when they were feasting him for his greatness and genius he said rather whimsically and wistfully, "If Silicon had been a gas, I would have been a major general." Silicon wasn't a gas.

Take an oyster. From an evolutionary point of view, it is a mollusk; it is way down in the evolutionary scale by millions of years. When a grain of sand gets into an oyster, it has a liability and it wiggles attempting to expel the liability. An oyster has a brain one millionth as big as a pin head. Instinct causes it to wiggle out the grain of sand. It usually succeeds. But when it fails to get rid of a liability like a grain of sand, it clamps down, closes up and converts that liability into a precious pearl. Converting liabilities into assets! Handicaps.

I am thinking now of obstacles. A long way back there was a man named Demosthenes. You remember him? Demosthenes couldn't speak. When he dreamed, he dreamed of a mighty audience in front of him, and in his dream felt that by the sheer inflection of his voice, he could make strong men cry one moment and laugh the next. Then he awakened and found that it was not a dream but a nightmare—he couldn't talk. It was before the day of apartment houses and yet the neighbors found fault with the noises that he made when he tried to speak. So Demosthenes went down to the seashore where there were no people. He saw pebbles lying on the shore and the strange idea came to him— he didn't have enough liabilities! He felt that if he just filled up his mouth with pebbles and, if he could talk just as well with a mouth full of pebbles—he couldn't talk worse—maybe by removing one of the pebbles each week, he would learn how to speak. Need I tell you that Demosthenes became not one of the greatest, but in all likelihood, the greatest orator of all time? You wouldn't say to me, *"In spite* of his handicap?" Nay, *because* of his handicap!

Think for a moment of John Bunyan. He lived two hundred years ago in England. His religious and theological views were unconventional and because of the moral climate of the day he was thrust into prison. He was a tinker, a mender of pots and pans, and he left behind a wife and four daughters, one of whom was stone blind. They put him in Bedford jail for seven years where he had only dry bread for food, dirty water for drink and a stone for a pillow. He certainly had enough alibis if he wanted an alibi. But something happened to him, the humble tinker, became a great thinker and in the alchemy of his spirit it was transformed and transfused and transfigured into spiritual assets. He wrote *The Pilgrims' Progress,* one of the great religious classics of all times. *In spite* of his difficulties? Nay, *because* of his difficulties.

Think for a moment of Epictetus, a slave who fell into the hands of another slave. A former slave in the nature of things, becomes a vindictive master. That explains the Bibles insight, "Remember the stranger for ye were strangers in the land of Egypt." The master twisted his leg and as Epictetus was a Stoic, he did not wince. He twisted it just a little more and Epictetus said rather calmly, "If you twist it just a little more than that, it will break." And he gave it another jerk and there it broke! He lay there uncared for, week after week, month after month and year after year. During that time he composed what he called his "discourses," a great book on human ethics, the best antidote in the world to worry. He tells us himself in that book that sometimes he felt that his breast would split wide open and his heart leap out in ecstatic joy, because even though his body was in chains, his soul was free. *In spite* of his hardships? Nay, *because* of his hardships!

Some years ago I was asked to give a commencement address at one of the great western universities. I gave about sixteen that year and I could see diplomas walking in by themselves. The president of the university and I stood and watched the graduates as they marched in. As we stood there the president said to me: "Oh, if you could only have been here two years ago. What a great commencement we had."

I said, "Did you have a *good* speaker that year?"

He said, "Oh, something happened, I wish you could have witnessed it; I could hardly believe what I saw."

And I asked, "Just what was it?"

Said he, "Four years earlier a little clump of flesh that called himself a student came to us; we didn't know whether to take him or not. The first week the professor of English said, 'When I call your name, rise, and after that I'll know you by name.' A name was called and no one rose; it was called a second time and still no one arose. The professor became just a bit indignant and said, 'Didn't I ask you to rise?' A voice chirped back, 'I'm sorry, sir, I haven't stood on my feet since I am two years old.' The four years passed and that little clump of flesh had won every honor that the university had ever bestowed. When the football captain had got his diploma, people applauded; when the baseball captain got his diploma, people applauded; when the Phi Beta Kappas got their diplomas, nobody applauded; then a name was called, and the football captain and the baseball captain made a basket out of their arms and they took this little clump of humanity and carried him across the stage." Then the president said to me, "The applause was so deafening that the walls began to tremble and the chandeliers began to swing. Dr. Mann, I have never witnessed anything like that in all my life."

It isn't what happens to *us*, its what happens *within us* that really counts.

Some of you may remember my "friend" Socrates. He had a great liability. He had "matrimonial indigestion." Do you know what that is? His wife didn't agree with him. She nagged and nagged and nagged, till she got tired nagging and then she scolded till she got tired scolding and then she started to nag all over again. Some men go out and get drunk and others jump into the river under such conditions. Socrates went out on the street. He couldn't even get a "thin" word in "edgewise" at home and so he talked to everybody on the street. When a man said, "Socrates, its a nice day," he asked, "What do you mean by a 'nice day.'? If it were this way every day, we'd all starve to death. The umbrella man would go broke." Then he would go to another man and finally they accused him of being the brightest man in the whole community and he said, "I plead guilty. I'm the brightest man that ever lived. I *know* that I know nothing and I've met no one that knows that much." Converting liabilities into assets!

Abraham Lincoln came from down in Kentucky where I come from. No books and no libraries and no schools! His father, though authors have tried to smooth it over, was just an old drunk. His mother was a remarkable woman. She died when he was nine years old. He always called her his "angel mother." He went into business and spent seventeen years to pay off the debts of a worthless partner for which he was not legally responsible, but took on the moral responsibility. He fell in love with a beautiful girl and became engaged to her. She died. He ran for the legislature and was defeated. He tried for the land office and didn't get it; he ran for the United States Senate and was defeated. One defeat after another but in the alchemy of the spirit that man grew and grew until he became what I truly believe to have been the greatest American of all time. Converting liabilities into assets!

I close with this illustration. A little boy lived in Edinburgh. He had trouble with his leg, so he went to the doctor. The doctor said he couldn't help him but that there was only one doctor who could and he lived in London. It was before the days of the "rule of thumb"—hitch-hiking. So he rode on the train part of the way, he tried to walk on his poor leg part of the way, and in the last stretch he crawled on his stomach like a worm. The doctor saw him and said that one of the legs would have to be amputated immediately, but that he would try to save the other. He lay on a bed week after week and month after month without a smile from anyone save from those angels in white, sometimes called "nurses." Then a great day came, there was to be an international meeting of great physicians. Twelve world specialists were brought in to examine him, to see if thy could save that other leg. While they were out in consultation, he reached over to one of the beds and got a stub of a pencil and then reached out to another bed and got a piece of wrapping paper and there wrote these lines. The moment I begin them, you will know that I am talking of the "Invictus" by William Ernest Henley:

> Out of the night that covers me,
>   Black as the pit from pole to pole,
> I thank whatever gods may be
>   For my unconquerable soul.
>
> In the fell clutch of circumstance
>   I have not winced nor cried aloud,
> Under the bludgeonings of chance
>   My head is bloody, but unbowed.
>
> Beyond this place of wrath and tears
>   Looms but the Horror of the shade,
> And yet the menace of the years
>   Finds and shall find me unafraid.
>
> It matters not how strait the gate,
>   How charged with punishments the scroll,
> I am the master of my fate;
>   I am the captain of my soul.

"Invictus." Unconquerable, insuperable, indomitable. Not what happens *to us,* but in the divine alchemy of the spirit transfused, transformed, transfigured, what happens *within* us. Invictus—unconquerable!

A RELIGION FOR NOW [8]

NATHAN M. PUSEY [9]

President Nathan M. Pusey of Harvard University gave this address at the opening convocation of the Harvard Divinity School, in Andover Chapel, at noon, on Wednesday, September 30, 1953. For the first time in almost half a century a president of Harvard had participated in the exercises at that school.

The Divinity School address took its title and its theme from President Charles Eliot's address, "The Religion of the Future," given in 1909 before this same theological school.

Dr. Pusey's thesis was that religion as expounded by Eliot was a diffused activity expressed in increased knowledge and good works, but without a full "consciousness" of "spiritual experiences" that were of a "sacred character." The speaker argued that the needs of 1953 called for religion as a "central area of human experience." To him the current scene was one of "very widespread religious illiteracy and corresponding little religious practice." Imperative, therefore, according to Pusey, was a study of religion in colleges and the responsibility of schools of religion "to do something fresh and convincing to meet the present need." Harvard Divinity School was pictured as a revitalized school of religion, not a peripheral unit, but a source of "increasing influence throughout the whole university."

The intellectual cast of this discourse is well ordered and mature. Its philosophical and theological assumptions are open to question by those critics who with varying degrees of dissent trace their origin of individualism to Ralph Waldo Emerson and his Divinity School address of July 15, 1838.

The speaker here closely adopted his language to his theological audience. Although he followed his manuscript closely, he had much animation of voice and bodily activity. His tones were pleasantly resonant; his articulation and pronunciation those of his Midwest. As speaker he had more vocal variety and platform liveliness than did his predecessor at Harvard, Dr. Conant.

Dr. Pusey was inaugurated on October 1, 1953, as the twenty-fourth president of Harvard.

[8] President Nathan Pusey furnished the text and granted permission for this reprint.

[9] For biographical note, see Appendix.

Members of the Faculty and of the Student Body of the Divinity School:

I am grateful to your acting dean, and to all of you, for this opportunity to meet and worship with you here in the Divinity School at the outset of a new academic year and at the beginning of my career as president of the university of which we are all members. I should like to admit at once by way of qualification, before I say anything else, that I know very little—almost nothing—as yet about you or your program—about your achievements, your aspirations, or your frustrations; but I hope to learn a good deal about these things as time goes on. I hope, too, to find ways to work constructively with you to bring this school closer to our heart's best desire; and I hope to play whatever part I can in such a way that I shall continue to be as welcome here in your company in the future as you have made me feel today.

As I was not prepared for my election to the presidency of Harvard near the close of the last academic year, so was I quite unready for the hundreds of congratulatory, and also often admonitory, letters which at once began to flood in upon me from all sorts and conditions of men, from all parts of the country, and even from abroad. Most of these—I can almost say, all of them—proved to be very welcome, but some of them were also disturbing because of the certainty and forcefulness, perhaps even the impetuosity and indignation—with which they pointed out things, sometimes even conflicting things, which were said urgently to be needed at Harvard, and about which I knew nothing.

No alleged shortcoming of the university was more frequently, nor more insistently, called to my attention than what was referred to as "the present low estate of religion at Harvard." A good many of my correspondents also spoke with feeling about what they called "the neglected condition of the Divinity School." It is of these two things that I wish to speak to you briefly today. A word about the latter first.

I am sure the case for neglect of this institution can and has been overstated, but were an outsider simply to glance at their physical facilities, their budgets, enrollments, sizes of faculties, and the like, it does seem irrefutable that for one reason or another more has been done for schools devoted to other of the great intellectual concerns of mankind—for medicine, law, and business, for example—than for the Divinity School. And it will surely, therefore, be encouraging to you, as it is to me, to know that there is at present a considerably quickened interest among members of the governing boards, alumni, and others to correct this apparent imbalance. Some important preliminary steps have already been taken, and other more considerable advances may be expected to follow in the future. I am sure we who are here today shall all welcome whatever is done in this direction. But now I want to talk rather about the other, the wider consideration, the alleged "present low estate of religion at Harvard" and of your relationship to this. I shall have to come to my point in rather a roundabout way.

Mr. Williams called our attention in introducing me to the fact that the last participation by a President of the University in an exercise of the Divinity School was in 1909. He had mentioned this to me earlier in inviting me to speak here today and I was immediately curious to see what this presidential valedictory had been like, and so got hold of it and read it. It was the address President Eliot gave at the close of the Eleventh Session of the Harvard Summer School of Theology in July, 1909, an address entitled "The Religion of the Future." I do not know how familiar this is to you, but I shall need to refer to it to make one or two comments about our present situation and opportunity.

In the first place, President Eliot's address suggests at least one reply to those people who have been insisting on Harvard's neglect of religion. For if one were to define religion as he apparently did, it is abundantly clear that this university was not, never has been, and is not now, irreligious at all. On the contrary.

There is evidence for President Eliot's own deep personal faith, and its nobility, in every line of his address, and it is possible—indeed it seems to me probable—that this faith not only animated many of the people at work in the university in his time, but that it had done so for a long time both before and after, and that much of the university's present great stature is owed to it. For example, he said in 1909:

The new religion will foster powerfuly a virtue which is comparativey new in the world—the love of truth and the passion for seeking it.

And again:

The workman today, who gets cut or bruised by a rough or dirty instrument, goes to a surgeon, who applies an antiseptic dressing to the wound, and prevents the poisoning. That surgeon is one of the ministers of the new religion. When dwellers in a slum suffer the familiar evils caused by overcrowding, impure food, and cheerless labor, the modern true believers contend against the sources of such misery by providing public baths, playgrounds, wider and cleaner streets, better dwellings, and more effective schools—that is, they attack the sources of physical and moral evil.

The word "moral" is slipped in rather unexpectedly at the end here, and it may carry the argument a bit too far, but despite this, there can be no doubt that President Eliot was a sincere and fervent believer in a religion that placed its greatest reliance on increased knowledge and good works. And I suspect further, as I have said, that a similar faith was widely held by members of this university in the period before the first World War when it was probably closer to an earlier Christian conviction than it was later to be, and that it has been held by many ever since. Judged by its fruits it has surely proved no inconsiderable faith, for it manifestly released, or at least expressed, a strong creative force that has been productive of much good both within the university and outside, and it seems to me beyond question, as I have said, that the present greatness of this university springs in no small measure from it. And yet I think it is no less true that by itself, this faith will no longer do.

We might quarrel endlessly over the relationship between humanitarianism and high religion. There would be no profit in this for us today. Let me then just state the following as a personal conviction, and go on: that though our predecessors in President Eliot's generation were unquestionably men of great faith, their faith will not do for us, if for no other reason, because events of the twentieth century have made its easy optimism unpalatable. For example, the passage about the passion for truth quoted above continued, "and the truth will progressively make men free; so that the coming generations will be freer, and therefore more productive and stronger than the preceding." We are not quite so sure about this as they were and it is this uncertainty itself which constitutes our present greatest problem.

It is not that we do not have faith, or at least want to have faith, but that certainty escapes us, and that all things have been brought into doubt, and that fearing to be victimized we are inclined not to believe at all. We simply are not the "true believers" of whom President Eliot spoke, and this suggests that his was not a religion for the future, but that something was left out of it which has now gone a long way toward vitiating his position, and which we must hold of again in the midst of our present difficulties, if we are to get on.

For President Eliot the enemies to his true faith were churches, creeds, priests, anything supernatural, any concern for a life after death, anything that professed to be sacramental. I suspect, for example—though I do not know this—that he would have considered the doctrine central to generations of believers, that Christ came into the world to save sinners, as so much twaddle. His was to be a "simple and rational faith" and there was to be no place in it for "metaphysical complexities or magical rites."

We may overlook the disparaging conjunction of unequal things in the last phrase, and observe simply that such things were not so easily to be gotten rid of: churches and creeds and metaphysical complexities persist, and we have need of them still. There has been ample time since 1909 to discover that you cannot get rid of things of this kind, or at least of the needs from which they spring, simply by turning your back on them or by pretending that they are not there. This is where President Eliot may have been wrong, at least wrong for our time, for it has now become frighteningly clear that if you try to ignore metaphysical considerations (I would say consideration of ultimate things) or cover them up in bursts of energy, they will rise up in perverted and distorted forms to mock one's thus too-circumscribed efforts. Nor was it right to have assumed, as President Eliot did, that if only one could get rid of churches and creeds, one would by that act also get rid of the human failings which had in the first place produced the blemishes irritating to him. Churchmen are not the only men who can be guilty of failures of imagination, understanding, and charity.

President Eliot had a creed, whether he admitted to it or not. It is there implicit in every line of his address. But in our time most of us will find this an inadequate one. What this proves, I think, is that our need was not then and is not now to get rid of creeds, but rather to examine into them, and now again, more especially, to find an adequate one for our time. We need to know, but we need also to believe, and what we want especially to do is to believe knowingly and to know with conviction.

President Eliot apparently would not, or could not, recognize that the old forms of Christianity which he was so ready to depreciate and which, as they had been latterly abused, rightfully irritated him, had at one time been vehicles for holding and transmitting truth, that is, for communicating profound and relevant insights about the human situation, from one generation to another. And what he did not suspect was that in getting rid of the forms we ordinary citizens would also run the risk of getting rid of the insights, and that we would, in fact, then in surrendering to a new kind of blindness or idolatry, run the risk of cutting ourselves off from a whole, possibly even the most central, area of human experience. He was wrong, I think, in urging his generation to get rid of what he called "paganized Christianity" by eschewing metaphysics and by escaping into a formless empyrean of good will. It would have been better to have exhorted them, rather, while keeping a firm grasp on the spiritual treasure that had been transmitted to them, to wrestle more vigorously toward a fresh understanding of "first things." At any rate it seems to me *we* must do this. For our need is not for a religion for the future but for religion now, for the vigorous and creative faith which Eliot and his generation has had in considerable measure spent its force, and in many areas, in many minds, a paralyzing disbelief has taken its place. A new effort of the human mind and heart and will is thus called for, and this, it seems to me, is where you—in this school and schools of this kind—come in.

For, "if the trumpet give an uncertain sound, who shall prepare himself to the battle?"

Out of our present great need a renewal must come. I do not mean to imply that we can lift ourselves by our own boot straps, but I am ready to insist that we can now study in areas too long neglected, can at least a little relax our wills and our zealotry, and can learn again to listen and to let ourselves be helped.

It has been my experience that when one inquires today about religious questions—at least outside professional circles—one is apt normally to be met with disinterest, ignorance, and apathy on the one hand, and too often where interest does exist, with ignorance and fanaticism on the other. We have not been well taught about religion, and there is as a consequence a very widespread religious illiteracy and correspondingly little religious practice. Perhaps as pupils we have been inclined to be unteachable. But I do not want to slip into President Eliot's error here by seeming to imply that all that is lacking is knowledge. It is rather, I think, faith.

Personal religion, and understanding of, and participation in, the work of the Church, could apparently in many earlier generations be taken for granted. Latterly they have tended to ebb away in the all but universal adoration of the State, and in almost idolatrous preoccupation with the secular order, the accumulation of knowledge, and with good works. There is not, and cannot be, a quarrel with any of these things in themselves, but only with the notion that they are independently sufficient goods. And it is because they have been tried and the people are still not fed, that you especially are now presented with an immense new and most difficult responsibility.

There is an almost desperate urgency for this and for other schools of religion now vigorously to do something fresh and convincing to meet the present need. It is leadership in religious knowledge, and even more, in religious experience—not increased industrial might, not more research facilities, certainly not these things by themselves—of which we now have a most gaping need. And it is because of this that you who have chosen to study religion and to give your lives to the ministry stand again where many times before your illustrious predecessors have stood in the very center of the fight. Andover Hall is not on the periphery of Harvard University; it is not remote from any region where the serious business of men is done—and it cannot be permitted to become so.

Harvard was begun at least in part, as you know, because our earliest predecessors were afraid lest they leave an illiterate ministry behind them. Certainly no one is going, or ever intended, to argue for an illiterate ministry; but if we think as Eliot did of all who do the world's work as ministers, regardless of what they know or care for God, perhaps that is what we have been getting. Our more immediate predecessors were inclined to think you can serve God through many careers other than that of the formal ministry. In this they were completely right. But it does not necessarily follow that in these other careers, any more than in the formal ministry itself, one necessarily serves God. We need to know what we are doing and how best to do it. And here again we all have need of you.

It is my very sincere hope therefore that theological studies can here be given a fresh impetus and a new life within this university. It is to be hoped, too, that such an augmented effort in this direction will result in more able and dedicated young men's coming into the ministry behind you, and that a changing climate of opinion will then make it possible for you who have chosen this path to lead fully significant and effective lives in a new and more Christian society.

Theology should not be thought of as a minor intellectual exercise among other intellectual exercises—certainly not only this. It is expected to carry an answer to our deepest hungers and need. You are here to grow in the knowledge, but also the love of God, and you should leave these halls with a will steadfastly to help others to do the same.

I do not wish to argue that there is any Christian truth different from truth itself. But it is necessary to recognize that truth can be lost in a formless and uninformed faith, and that we can no longer get along in the face of our present great needs with such. The university must always serve truth, but we must make a fresh effort and learn again to do this more fully. Eliot's insight did not encompass the whole of it; another man's will not either, but we must go on trying, freshly and creatively, in humility and in love, and with all the allies we can find. It is to be hoped, therefore, that we can now here have a revitalized school of religious learning, and that its influence will be increasingly felt throughout the whole university.

A member of your faculty said here a few years ago that, "Faith is the consciousness that moral values and spiritual experiences have a sacred character"—"faith is the consciousness that moral values and spiritual experiences have a *sacred* character." It is more of this consciousness that we most desperately need, and that, difficult as it may seem to be epistemologically, we must learn again to know by faith with thanksgiving. There are many who will join with me in the hope expressed here today that in this effort Harvard—especially the faculty and the graduates of this school—will again lead the way.

APPENDIX

BIOGRAPHICAL NOTES

AIKEN, GEORGE DAVID (1892-   ). Born, Dummeston, Vermont; graduate, Brattleboro, Vermont, High School, 1909; school director, Town of Putney, 1920-37; State House of Representatives, 1930-33; Speaker of House, 1933-34; Lieutenant Governor of Vermont, 1935-37, Governor of Vermont, 1937-41; United States Senator from Vermont since 1940; author of *Speaking from Vermont* and other books; Republican. (See also *Current Biography*: 1947.)

BENSON, EZRA TAFT (1899-   ). Born, Whitney, Idaho; Utah State Agricultural College, 1918-21; B.S., Brigham Young University. 1926; M.S., Iowa State College, 1927; graduate study, University of California, 1937-38; operated farm, Idaho, 1923-29; in British Isles and Europe, Mission for Church of Jesus Christ Latter Day Saints, 1921-23; University of Idaho Extension Service, 1930-38; executive secretary, National Council of Farmer Cooperatives, 1939-44; executive officer, American Institute of Cooperation, 1943-53: prominent offices in Church of the Latter Day Saints; appointed Secretary of Agriculture in Eisenhower's cabinet, January 1953. (See also *Current Biography: 1953.*)

BRICKER, JOHN WILLIAM (1893-   ). Born, Madison County, Ohio; A.B., Ohio State University, 1916, LL.B., 1920; Admitted, Ohio bar, 1917; Assistant Attorney General of Ohio, 1923-27, Attorney General, 1933-37; Governor of Ohio, 1939-45; Republican candidate for vice president, 1944; United States Senator from Ohio since 1945; First Lieutenant, United States Army, World War I; member Delta Sigma Rho, Order of Coif and other honorary and professional societies. (See also *Current Biography*: 1943.)

BROWNELL, HERBERT, JR. (1904-   ). Born, Peru, Nebraska; A.B., University of Nebraska, 1924; LL.B. Yale Law School, 1927; Admitted to New York bar, 1927; law practice in New York; past chairman, Republican National Committee; campaign manager, Dewey-Warren ticket, 1948; appointed United States Attorney General in Eisenhower cabinet, 1953. Phi Beta Kappa, Sigma Delta Chi, Order of Coif, and other honorary societies; co-author of *Manual of New York Hotel and Restaurant Law*. (See also *Current Biography: 1944*.)

BUTLER, HUGH (1878-1954). Born, Missouri Valley, Iowa; student, Doane Academy, 1896; B.S., Doane College, 1900, LL.D., 1940; successively engineer, grain and feed miller, director of Nebraska Consolidated Mills; president, Grain and Feed Dealers National Association, 1929-30; United States Senator from Nebraska from 1941 until his sudden death in July 1954. Republican. (See also *Current Biography: 1950*.)

DAVIS, ELMER HOLMES (1890-   ). Born, Aurora, Indiana; A.B., Franklin College, 1910; A.M., 1911; Rhodes Scholar, Oxford University, A.B., 1912; L.H.D., Wabash College, 1942, LL.D., St. Lawrence University, 1946, and other honorary degrees; staff of the New York *Times*, 1914-24; news analyst Columbia Broadcasting System, 1939-42; director of Office of War Information, 1942-45; President, Authors League, 1939-41; news analyst, American Broadcasting Company since 1945; author of *But We Were Born Free*, 1954, and many volumes of fiction and essays. (See also *Current Biography: 1940.)*

DULLES, JOHN FOSTER (1888-   ). Born, Washington, D.C.; B.A., Princeton University, 1908, LL.D., 1946; Sorbonne, Paris, 1908-09; LL.B., George Washington University, 1911; LL.D., Tufts College, Wagner College, Northwestern University; began law practice, New York City, 1911; director, Bank of New York; trustee, Rockefeller Foundation; chairman, Carnegie Endowment for International Peace; chairman, Federal Council of Churches Commission on a Just and Durable Peace; secretary, Hague Peace Conference, 1907; captain and major,

United States Army, 1917-18; member, Reparations Commission and Supreme Economic Council, 1919; member, United States delegation, San Francisco Conference on World Organization, 1945; Council of Foreign Ministers, London, 1945; General Assembly, United Nations, 1946; meeting of Council of Foreign Ministers, Moscow, 1947; London meeting of "Big Four," 1947; United States Senator appointed (Republican) from New York, July-November 1949 (to complete term of Senator Wagner); appointed counselor, Department of State, April 1950; appointed, with rank of ambassador, to negotiate terms of peace for Japan, 1951; representative at signing of Japanese peace treaty, San Francisco, 1951; writer and speaker on international affairs; authors of *War or Peace,* 1950; appointed Secretary of State in the Eisenhower cabinet, 1953. (See also *Current Biography: 1949.*)

EISENHOWER, DWIGHT D. (1890-   ). Born, Denison, Texas; B.S., United States Military Academy, 1915; Army Tank School, 1921; graduate, War College, 1929; Second Lieutenant, United States Army, 1915; Lieutenant Colonel, Tank Corps, World War I; advanced through grades to General of the Army, December 1944; Chief of Operations Division, Office of Chief of Staff, 1942; Commanding General, European Theatre of Operations, June 1942; Allied Commander in Chief, North Africa, November 1942; Supreme Commander of Allied Land, Sea, and Air Forces in Western Europe, November 1943; Chief of Staff, United States Army, 1945-48; President of Columbia University, 1948-52; appointed Supreme Commander of the North Atlantic Treaty Nations, 1950; entered in presidential primaries on Republican ticket, January 1952; author of *Crusade in Europe,* 1948, *Eisenhower Speaks,* 1948; elected President of the United States, November 1952. (See also *Current Biography: 1948.*)

EVANS, LOUIS HADLEY (1897-   ). Born, Goshen, Indiana; A.B., Occidental College, 1918, D.D., 1944; B.D., McCormick Theological Seminary, 1922; D.D., Jamestown College, Washington and Jefferson College, John Brown University, and other institutions; ordained, Presbyterian Ministry, 1922, minister Westhope, North Dakota, 1922-25; Wilmington, California, 1925-28; Pomona, California, 1928-31; Pittsburgh, 1931-41; Hollywood, 1941-53; since May, 1953, Minister at Large, Presbyterian Church in the U.S.A.; lecturer at many colleges and universites; officer in many religious and philanthropic organizations; served with navy, World War I; author of *Youth Seeks a Master*, 1941; *Give us a Voice*, 1939; and other books.

FAIRLESS, BENJAMIN F. (1890-   ). Born, Pigeon Run, Ohio; student, Wooster College; graduated in civil engineering, Ohio Northern University, 1913; honorary D.Sc., Kent State University, University of Pittsburgh; D.Eng., Ohio Northern University, Stevens Institute of Technology; civil engineer, Wheeling and Lake Erie Railroad, 1913; with Central Steel Company, successively civil engineer, mill superintendent, general superintendent, vice president in charge of operations, 1913-26; vice president and general manager, United Alloy Steel, 1926-28; president and general manager, 1928-30; executive vice president, Republic Steel Corporation, 1930-35; president Carnegie Illinois Steel Corporation, 1935-37; president and director, United States Steel Corporation, since 1938. (See also *Current Biography: 1942.*)

HENNINGS, THOMAS CAREY, JR. (1903-   ). Born, St. Louis; A.B., Cornell University, 1924; LL.B., Washington University, 1926; admitted to bar, 1926; Representative from Missouri, United States Congress, 1935-41; Lieutenant Commander, United States Navy, 1941-43; circuit court attorney for St. Louis district, 1940-41, 1943-45; private practice, 1945-50; United States Senator from Missouri, 1950; member of many civic and professional organizations, Democrat.

HOBBY, OVETA CULP (Mrs. William P. Hobby) (1905-   ). Born, Killeen, Texas; educated public schools and private tutors; student, Mary Hardin Baylor College; LL.D., Baylor University, Sam Houston State Teachers College, University of Chattanooga, and other honorary degrees; various editorial positions with

Houston Post, 1931-38; later director and executive vice president; appointed director, Woman's Army Auxiliary Corps May, 1942; director, Women's Army Corps 1943-45; many governmental and executive posts, and boards of various private charitable organizations; appointed Secretary of Health, Education and Welfare in Eisenhower cabinet, January 1953; author of *Mr. Chairman*, and syndicated column with this title. (See also *Current Biography*: *1942*.)

HOOVER, HERBERT CLARK (1874-   ). Born, West Branch, Iowa; B.A. in engineering, Stanford University, 1895; honorary degrees from Brown University, Columbia University, Johns Hopkins University, Oxford University, University of Prague, and other institutions here and abroad; United States Food Administrator, 1917-19; director of various relief organizations for the war-stricken nations of Europe; appointed Secretary of Commerce in 1921; Republican President of the United States, 1929-33; coordinator of food supplies to thirty-eight countries, 1946; chairman of Committee on Organization of the Executive Branch of the Government, 1947-49; member Advisory Board, World Bank Reconstruction and Development; appointed chairman of Committee on Government Operations, July 1953; author of *American Individualism*, 1922; *The Challenge to Liberty*, 1934; *Addresses Upon the American Road*, 1948-50; and numerous addresses on government. (See also *Current Biography*: *1943*.)

HUMPHREY, GEORGE M. (1890-   ). Born, Sheboygan, Michigan; LL.B. University of Michigan, 1912; law practice, Saginaw, Michigan, 1911-18, general attorney, M.A. Hanna Co. (steel manufacturers), Cleveland, Ohio, 1918, president since 1921; director of many subsidiaries or affiliated companies, including Phelps Dodge Corporation, Iron Ore Company of Canada, National City Bank; appointed Secretary of the Treasury in the Eisenhower cabinet, January 1953. (See also *Current Biography*: *1953*.)

JOHNSTON, ERIC ALLEN (1896-   ). Born, Washington, D.C.; soon moved to Spokane, Washington; LL.B., University of

Washington, 1917; Captain, United States Marine Corps, 1917-22; entered business 1922; later co-owner and president of large electrical contracting and manufacturing companies; president, Spokane Chamber of Commerce, 1931-32; director, United States Chamber of Commerce, 1943, vice president, 1941, president, 1942-46 (four terms); visited South America, Great Britain, and Russia, 1943; president, Motion Picture Association of America 1945-50; member, Publicity Advisory Board, Economic Cooperation Administration, 1948; Administrator, Economic Stabilization Agency, 1950-52; Chairman, International Development Advisory Board since 1952; author of *America Unlimited*, 1944 (See also *Current Biography: 1943.*)

KENNAN, GEORGE FROST (1904-   ). Born, Milwaukee; A.B. Princeton University, 1925; foreign consular service during the next twenty-seven years, including posts at Hamburg, Riga, Berlin, Vienna, Prague; minister-counselor, Moscow, 1945; National War College, Washington, 1948; policy planning staff, Department of State, 1947; ambassador to Moscow, 1952; resigned, 1953. (See also *Current Biography: 1947.*)

LEWIS, JOHN LLEWELLYN. (1880-   ). Born, Lucas, Iowa; educated public schools; legislative agent, United Mine Workers of America, 1909-11; representative, American Federation of Labor, 1911-17; president, United Mine Workers of America, since 1920; formerly president, Congress of Industrial Organizations; served on various government commissions, and agencies. (See also *Current Biography: 1942.*)

MANN, LOUIS LEOPOLD (1890-   ). Born, Louisville, Kentucky; graduated from Louisville High School, 1907; student, Johns Hopkins University, 1907-08; B.A., University of Cincinnati, 1910, M.A., 1912; B.L.H., Hebrew Union College, 1911; ordained rabbi, 1914; Ph.D., Yale University, 1920; D.D., Hebrew Union College, 1944; D.S.Th., Northwestern University, 1949; rabbi, Chicago Sinai Congregation, since 1923; lecturer, Department of Oriental languages, University of Chicago, since 1924; executive officer or board member of many charitable, religious, and professional organizations and governmental agencies; contributor to various encyclopedias; contributor to *Best Sermons*, 1944.

MARSHALL, THURGOOD (1908-   ). Born, Baltimore; attended Negro elementary and high schools in Baltimore; attended Lincoln University (Pennsylvania); graduate of Howard University Law School, 1933; director and counsel, Legal Defense and Educational Fund of the National Association for Advancement of Colored People, since 1938; has argued cases before the United States Supreme Court, on Negro rights; in legal work has visited every state, and Japan and Korea.

MEANY, GEORGE (1894-   ). Born New York City; attended elementary and high schools, New York City; journeyman plumber, 1915; business representative, Plumbers Local Union, 1922-34; president, New York State Federation of Labor, 1934-39; secretary-treasurer, American Federation of Labor, 1940-1952; elected president American Federation of Labor, November 25, 1952. (See also *Current Biography*: *1942*.)

PUSEY, NATHAN M. (1907-   ). Born, Council Bluffs, Iowa; graduate Abraham Lincoln High School, 1924; A.B., Harvard University, 1928, A.M., 1932, Ph.D., 1937; LL.D., Wesleyan University, 1944, LL.D., Ripon College, 1945, L.H.D., Coe College, 1948; tutor, Lawrence College, 1935-38; assistant professor, history, Scripps College, 1938-40; assistant professor, classics, Wesleyan University, 1940-43; associate professor, 1943-44; president Lawrence College, 1944-53; inaugurated president of Harvard University, October 13, 1953. Member, Phi Beta Kappa. (See also *Current Biography*: *1953*.)

STEVENSON, ADLAI EWING (1900-   ). Born, Los Angeles; A.B., Princeton University, 1922; J.D., Northwestern University Law School, 1926; LL.D., Illinois Wesleyan University, Northwestern University, Bradley University; reporter, *Daily Pantagraph* (Bloomington, Illinois), 1924-25; admitted to Illinois bar, 1926; member, Chicago law firms, 1927-41; assistant to Secretary of Navy, 1941-44; chief, Foreign Economic Administrations, Italy missions, 1943; assistant to Secretary of State, 1945; adviser, United States delegation, General Assembly of United Nations, London, 1946; United States delegate, General Assembly of United Nations, New York, 1946, 1947; governor of Illinois, 1948-52; Democratic candidate for president, 1952; tour around the world, 1953. (See also *Current Biography*: *1949*.)

WARREN, EARL (1891-   ). Born, Los Angeles; B.L., University of California, 1912, J.D., 1914; LL.D., University of Redlands, University of Southern California, Santa Clara University, College of Pacific, Cornell College, Union College and other institutions; admitted to California bar, 1914, practiced law, San Francisco and Oakland, 1914-17; district attorney, Alameda County, 1925-39, Attorney General of California, 1939-43; Governor of California, 1943-52; Republican candidate for vice president, 1948; appointed Chief Justice, United States Supreme Court, 1953; First Lieutenant, United States Army, 1917-18; Captain, reserve until 1936; officer in various bar associations. (See also *Current Biography*: *1944, 1954*.)

CUMULATIVE AUTHOR INDEX

An author index to the volumes of *Representative American Speeches* for the years 1937-1938 through 1953-1954. The date following the title of each speech indicates the volume in which it appears.

SPEECH AND DEBATING

Competitive Debate: Rules and Strategy. By G. M. Musgrave. 151p. rev. ed. 1946. $1.25.

Democracy ~~Through~~ Discussion. By Bruno Las~~well~~. ~~315p.~~ 1949. ~~$3.50.~~

Discussion ~~Methods:~~ Illustrated. ~~By J. V.~~ Garland. ~~370p.~~ 3d ed. rev. ~~1951. $3.~~

Extempore S~~peaking: A~~ Handbook for the Student, the Coach, and the Judge. By D. L. Holley. 115p. 1947. $1.50.

High School Forensics: An Integrated Program. By A. E. Melzer. 153p. 1946. 90c.

How to Debate. By H. B. Summers, F. L. Whan, and T. A. Rousse. rev. ed. 349p. 1950. $2.75.

Representative American Speeches. By A. C. Baird, ed. Published annually in The Reference Shelf. Prices

Each volume contains representative speeches by eminent men and women on public occasions during the year. Each speech is prefaced by a short sketch of the speaker and the occasion.

Selected Readings in Rhetoric and Public Speaking. By Lester Thonssen, comp. 324p. 1942. $3.50.

THE REFERENCE SHELF *(Continued)*

Volume XXI

No.
2. Representative American Speeces: 1948-1949. A. C. Baird. $1.75.

Volume XX

No.
5. Federal World Government. J. E. Johnsen. $1.50.
6. Federal Information Controls in Peacetime. R. E. Summers. $1.50.

No.
7. Should the Communist Party Be Outlawed? J. E. Johnsen. $1.50.

Volume XIX

No.
3. Free Medical Care. C. A. Peters. $1.25.

No.
5. United Nations or World Government. J. E. Johnsen. 75c.

Volume XVIII

No.
3. Representative American Speeches: 1945-1946. A. C. Baird. $1.25.
5. Anatomy of Racial Intolerance. G. B. de Huszar. $1.25.

No.
6. Palestine: Jewish Homeland? J. E. Johnsen. $1.25

Volume XVII

No.
4. Representative American Speeches: 1943-1944. A. C. Baird. $1.25.

WITHDRAWN

Volume XVI

No.
1. Representative American Speeches: 1941-1942. A. C. Baird. $1.25.

No.
6. Representative American Speeches: 1942-1943. A. C. Baird. $1.25.

Volume XV

No.
1. Representative American Speeches: 1940-1941. A. C. Baird. $1.25.
2. Universal Military Service. R. E. Summers and H. B. Summers. $1.25.
3 Federal Regulation of Labor Unions. J. V. Garland. $1.25.

No.
7. The Closed Shop. J. E. Johnsen. $1.25.
9. Permanent Price Control Policy. J. E. Johnsen. $1.25.
10. A Federal Sales Tax. E. R. Nichols. $1.25.